YORK

John Harvey

B. T. Batsford Ltd
London and Sydney

By the same author:

Henry Yevele
Gothic England
The Plantagenets
Dublin
Tudor Architecture
The Gothic World
English Mediaeval Architects
A Portrait of English
   Cathedrals
The Cathedrals of Spain

Catherine Swynford's Chantry
The Master Builders
The Mediaeval Architect
Conservation of Buildings
Early Gardening Catalogues
Man the Builder
Cathedrals of England and
   Wales
Early Nurserymen
Mediaeval Craftsmen

Bibliographies:

English Cathedrals – A Reader's Guide
Conservation of Old Buildings
Early Horticultural Catalogues – A Checklist

Revised Muirhead's Blue Guides

Northern Spain   Southern Spain

Edited with translation:

William Worcestre: Itineraries (1478–1480)

First published 1975
© John Harvey 1975
ISBN 0 7134 2993 3

Printed and bound in Great Britain by
Richard Clay (The Chaucer Press), Ltd, Bungay, Suffolk
for the publishers B. T. Batsford Limited
4 Fitzhardinge Street, London W1H 0AH
and 23 Cross Street, Brookvale, N.S.W. 2100, Australia

Contents

Illustrations

Maps

Acknowledgements

The authors and publishers wish to thank the following for permission to reproduce the photographs included in this book: A. F. Kersting, F.R.P.S., plates 16, 19, 20, 23; the National Monuments Record, plates 2, 3, 9, 12, 13, 15, 17, 18, 21, 24, 25, 26, 27, 31, 32; the National Portrait Gallery, plate 34; the Science Museum, plates 4, 5; Mrs Olive Smith, plate 14; York City Art Gallery, plates 1, 35, 36, 37; York Public Library, plates 11, 22. Plate 33 is from the publisher's collection.

YORK

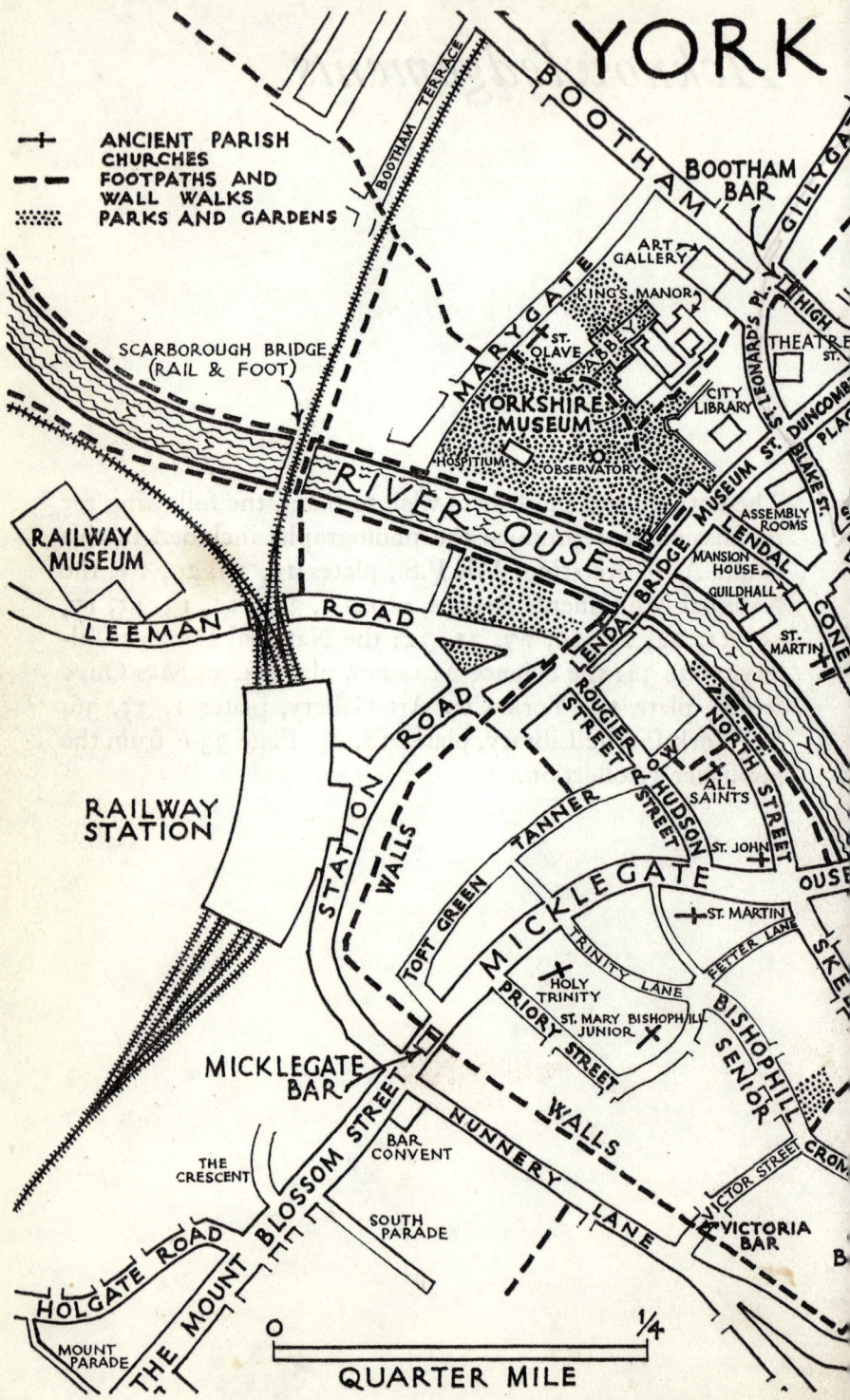

ANCIENT PARISH
CHURCHES
FOOTPATHS AND
WALL WALKS
PARKS AND GARDENS

BOOTHAM

BOOTHAM
BAR

GILLYGA

HIGH

BOOTHAM TERRACE

ART
GALLERY

KING'S MANOR

ST. LEONARD'S PL.

THEATRE
ST.

DUNCOM
PLAC

MARYGATE

ST.
OLAVE

ABBEY

CITY
LIBRARY

MUSEUM ST.

BLAKE ST.

SCARBOROUGH BRIDGE
(RAIL & FOOT)

YORKSHIRE
MUSEUM

HOSPITIUM

OBSERVATORY

ASSEMBLY
ROOMS

LENDAL

CONE

RIVER OUSE

LENDAL BRIDGE

MANSION
HOUSE

GUILDHALL

ST.
MARTIN

RAILWAY
MUSEUM

LEEMAN

ROAD

STATION ROAD

WALLS

TANNER

TOFT GREEN

ROUGIER
STREET

STREET

HUDSON
STREET

NORTH

STREET

ALL
SAINTS

ST. JOHN

OUSE

SKE

RAILWAY
STATION

MICKLEGATE

ST. MARTIN

FETTER LANE

TRINITY LANE

PRIORY

STREET

HOLY
TRINITY

ST. MARY BISHOPHILL
JUNIOR

BISHOPHILL

SENIOR

MICKLEGATE
BAR

BLOSSOM STREET

BAR
CONVENT

NUNNERY

WALLS

VICTOR STREET

CROM

VICTORIA
BAR

B

THE
CRESCENT

SOUTH
PARADE

LANE

HOLGATE ROAD

THE MOUNT

MOUNT
PARADE

O

1/4

QUARTER MILE

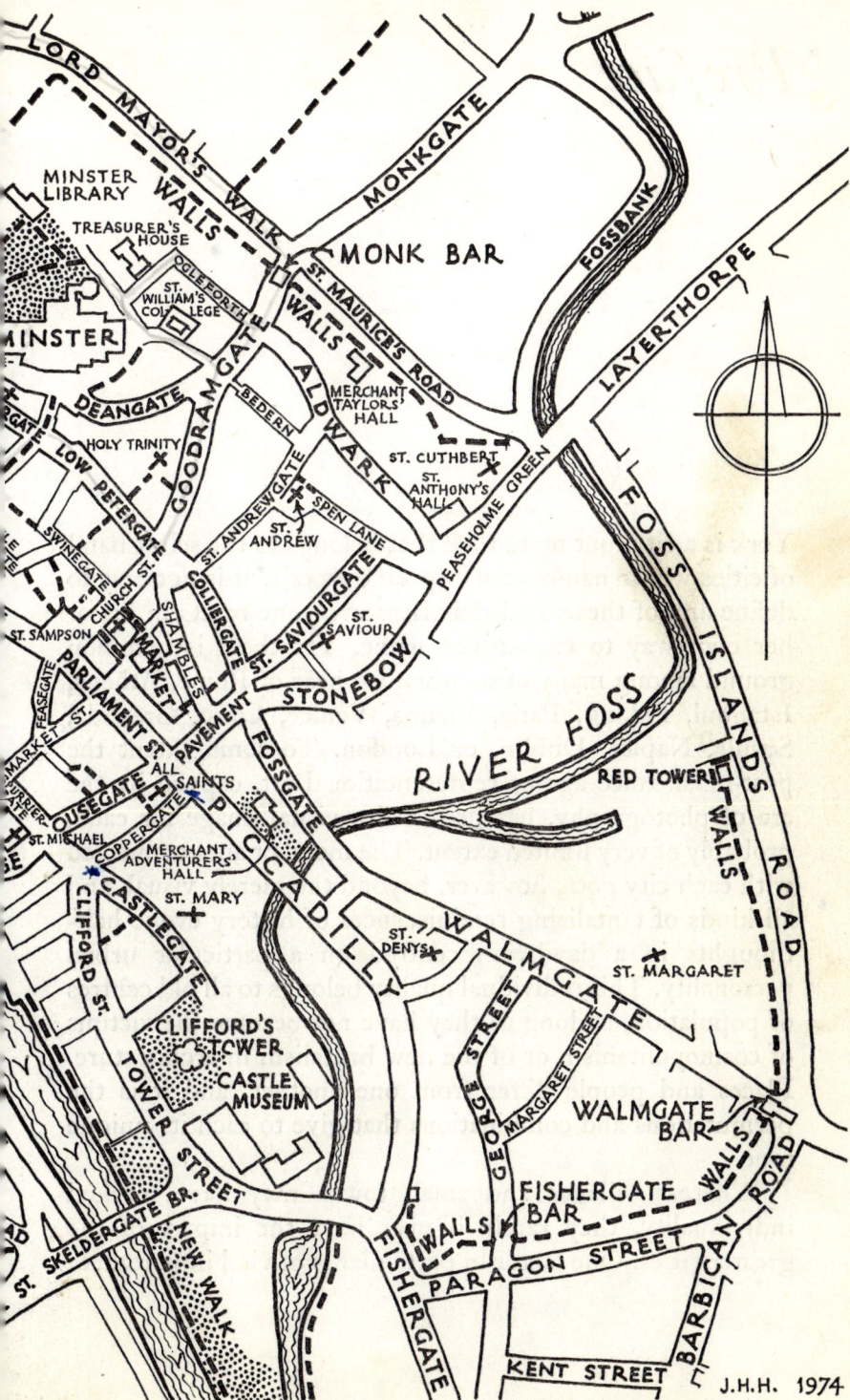

MINSTER LIBRARY

TREASURER'S HOUSE

MINSTER

ST. WILLIAM'S COLLEGE

OGLEFORTH

LORD MAYOR'S WALK

WALLS

MONKGATE

MONK BAR

FOSSBANK

LAYERTHORPE

ST. MAURICE'S ROAD

WALLS

MERCHANT TAYLORS' HALL

DEANGATE

GOODRAMGATE

ALDWARK

BEDERN

HOLY TRINITY

LOW PETERGATE

SWINEGATE

CHURCH ST.

ST. ANDREWGATE

ST. ANDREW

SPEN LANE

ST. CUTHBERT

ST. ANTHONY'S HALL

PEASEHOLME GREEN

ST. SAMPSON

COLLIERGATE

ST. SAVIOURGATE

ST. SAVIOUR

SHAMBLES

MARKET

PARLIAMENT ST.

FEASEGATE

PAVEMENT

STONEBOW

FOSSGATE

RIVER FOSS

FOSS ISLANDS ROAD

RED TOWER

WALLS

OUSEGATE

ALL SAINTS

COPPERGATE

ST. MICHAEL

PICCADILLY

MERCHANT ADVENTURERS' HALL

ST. MARY

CLIFFORD ST.

CASTLEGATE

ST. DENYS

WALMGATE

ST. MARGARET

GEORGE STREET

MARGARET STREET

CLIFFORD'S TOWER

CASTLE MUSEUM

TOWER STREET

WALMGATE BAR

FISHERGATE BAR

WALLS

BARBICAN ROAD

ST. SKELDERGATE BR.

NEW WALK

FISHERGATE

WALLS

PARAGON STREET

KENT STREET

J.H.H. 1974

Preface

York is a city, but more than that belongs to the select band of cities whose names evoke specific moods. It is not easy to define any of these, and doubtless everyone reacts in his or her own way to each given name. Yet there is common ground among many of us when we hear of Rome, Athens, Istanbul, Peking, Paris, Vienna, Venice, Cairo, Granada, Seville, Naples, Dublin, or London. To some extent the post-renaissance age of representational art, capped by the era of photography, has provided a visual image for each, probably of very limited extent. The mood or aura connected with each city goes, however, beyond the merely visual, and all kinds of tantalising reminiscences of history evoke half-thoughts in a daydream centred on a particular urban personality. This individual quality belongs to all old centres of population, so long as they have not become the victims of cosmopolitanism or of the new brutalism in architecture. Places and people differ from one another, and it is the permutations and combinations that give to each its unique tone.

Whereas villages and small towns may have marked individuality, they rarely if ever have the impact of the greater cities. One factor in particular is of vital importance:

that the city is or has been a capital. This capitality – to borrow a word from the Spanish *capitalidad* – is the essence of the true city. Its metropolitan status as a seat of government sets on it a more or less permanent mark. Though sometimes reduced to a faint ghost of its former self, in towns like Tamworth or villages such as Sherburn-in-Elmet, the former habit of command, of actual rule over an independent state, seems never to be quite effaced. A city in the fullest sense is therefore something more than a town which happens to possess the cathedral of a bishop, or to which the name of city has been granted by charter. It is the place from which sovereign mandates have issued, a throne-room enshrining the majesty within.

Travellers on the continent of Europe are often struck by this indefinable difference of atmosphere, marking off a great many large cities, notably in Germany, Italy, and Spain. For long periods and until comparatively recent times, these countries have had a substantial number of capitals, each the centre of a kingdom or a city-state on its own. There is no real likeness between the average English county town or cathedral city and places such as Toledo, Munich or Florence, Venice or Cordova. The same quality is present in places outside Europe and Christendom: Cairo, Damascus, Antioch, Konya, Fez. All are or have been over long periods the centres from which great kingdoms or empires have been governed, the nodal points at the centre each of a spider's web of political activity. For our present purpose it is enough to say that York belongs to this band; its place lies historically among the super-cities even though its centripetal magnetism may have run down and its glory have departed.

The interest of York is that, in England, its position is highly exceptional. So far as the kingdoms of the Saxon Heptarchy could be said to have capitals, only those of Kent (Canterbury) and Wessex (Winchester) preserved any relic of metropolitan status that could rival that of York, the chief city of Northumbria. Chichester, Colchester, Tamworth, and Thetford were never comparable centres of trade or population. Apart from London, the only pre-industrial cities comparable to York were Bristol, Coventry, Newcastle-upon-Tyne, and Norwich. So the cities of great prosperity and material importance were otherwise devoid of the status of capitals; while Canterbury and Winchester, after the Norman Conquest, were never near the first rank as major settlements. To add to this double eminence, York was actually the *de facto* capital of the whole country in 1298–1304 and again for 12 more years scattered in groups through the fourteenth century. York had been in pre-Conquest times the capital of an independent Viking kingdom from 875 to 954; and from 1537 it was for over a century the seat of the Council of the North, with control over the whole of northern England. Its position as spiritual capital of the whole of the enormous county of Yorkshire has never been challenged.

The factors which, taken together, give to York this pre-eminence are essential functions of its history, but it has other claims which are perhaps accidental. It has preserved, more or less complete, the circuit of its mediaeval ramparts and walls. So too have Chester and Chichester, but on a far smaller scale. The cathedral, York Minster, is the largest surviving mediaeval church in England in volume, and only marginally surpassed in overall area by Lincoln and equalled by Winchester. All three were exceeded by London's Old St Paul's, as might be expected. York Minster, however, also excels all other churches in the country in the amount of its original stained glass, preserved by the personal intervention of Fairfax when York fell to his arms in the Civil War. It was to Fairfax also that the relatively undamaged state of the churches, civic buildings and houses of the old city was due: a saving grace for which York has not been sufficiently grateful in later times. Yet, in spite of serious erosion, York has kept its walls, its Minster and many of its ancient buildings through the public spirit of its inhabitants and their love for their home.

The inhabitants of York, through the centuries, form an interesting study in themselves. York, like London and other capitals, has always exercised a power of attraction upon strangers, from other parts of England and from foreign countries. Many Yorkers, like Cockneys, are in and out in three generations, so that the population is continually changing. Yet there is a tradition of looking inwards, sus-pecting the outsider and wondering if he measures up to local standards, an attitude summarised in the tale of one citizen saying to another: 'There's a furriner on t'other side o' t' road; 'eave 'alf a brick at 'im an' see 'ow 'e takes it.' None the less, the great conflicts are those between the men in the street, regardless of origin, and their elected rulers. The stringent laws against speaking ill of the Mayor, so frequently invoked down the centuries, were not invented for nothing.

York is, then, both in its physical self and in its human dwellers a fit subject for study. This it has had in plenty during the last three centuries and a full bibliography of the city would be a considerable book in itself. To add another title to the pile may seem a rash proceeding; but the city is constantly changing, and there is perhaps room for the view of a resident outsider. For it is a striking fact that almost all books on York fall decisively into one of two classes: those written from inside, and those written with an external and objective viewpoint but with little understanding of the place itself. This applies particularly to works of serious research: they have depended either upon the documents accessible in York, or upon material elsewhere. This has occasionally been overcome by collaboration, as in the notable books of the late T. P. Cooper on the Walls of York and upon the Castle: Cooper, a brilliant and close observer, resident in the city, took pains to get help from authorities expert in the public records and other historical sources not locally available. On the other hand, the massive body of work produced by James Raine, chancellor of York Minster in the middle of last century, suffers from undue reliance on local documents; while the recent Victoria County History of the city, the collaborative work of a brilliant team of professional historians, betrays at many points an inadequacy of personal knowledge.

Two authors on York stand head and shoulders above the rest: Francis Drake and Robert Davies. Drake (1696–1771), who came of a clerical family, was city surgeon from 1727 and two years later began his great book *Eboracum*, completed and published in seven years. Elected Fellow of the Royal Society and of the Society of Antiquaries before the book was published, Drake was a truly outstanding scholar in the field of local studies, though handicapped by diffidence and by lifelong Toryism which eventually lost him his job with the Whig Corporation. Davies (1793–1875) was born in York, studied law, and was Town Clerk for 20 years from 1828. He was both an archivist before his time and a book-collector, and his work shows unusually wide learning, coupled with a gift of observation. Among the works published in his lifetime his *Memoir of the York Press* is notable as a detailed bibliographical study, but he is memorable above all for his lectures, issued posthumously as *Walks through the City of York* (1880). As a detailed study of local history, house by house and person by person, this has permanent and unique value besides showing Davies (in 1850–9, when the lectures were prepared) as an outstanding pioneer in a new field.

One other old book deserves not only commendation but the grateful thanks of every student of York and Yorkshire: the *Collectio Rerum Ecclesiasticarum de Dioecesi Eboracensi; or, Collections relative to Churches and Chapels within the Diocese of York* . . . (*and*) *Diocese of Ripon*, by George Lawton (1779–1869). Published in 1840 and re-issued with additions in 1842, the book remains authoritative. Not only does it contain full details of the history and endowments of every church and chapel within the ancient county but its introduction provides a detailed study of available original records, both local and in London, Oxford, and elsewhere, as well as many in private hands; and also of all printed works of relevance. The diligence and accuracy of Lawton's work are beyond praise and astonishing for his time.

During the last century a flood of books, and of editions of York records, has poured from the presses, some of the particularly significant items appearing in the bibliography (page 170). Here mention must be made of Robert Hardisty Skaife (1830–1916), nephew of Robert Davies and editor of many documents and compiler of an immense collection on all the civic officers of York, now in the City Library; of George Benson, a York architect (1856–1935), whose *Account of . . . York* in three parts (1911–25) is the best modern history in spite of inadequate references and poor index; Charles Brunton Knight, who provided a most valuable and fully indexed compendium in his *A History of the City of York* (1944); and Angelo Raine (1877–1962) who edited eight volumes of material from the York House Books and towards the end of his life published the summation of 35 years of work as Honorary Archivist to the city in *Mediaeval York* (1955). To these must be added one living writer, Mr Ronald Willis, whose *Portrait of York* (1972) is all that a portrait should be.

My own contacts with York and searches in its records now stretch back for over 30 years, and my continuous residence in the city for more than ten. My personal debt is correspondingly large: to the late David Black, Mrs N. K. M. Gurney, Lemuel Powell, Canon J. S. Purvis, Jeff Radley, and the Revd Angelo Raine; and among the living to

Mr C. B. L. Barr, Miss E. Brunskill, Mrs Jean Bryant, Dr R. M. Butler, Canon Reginald Cant, Professor R. R. Darlington, Dr R. B. Dobson, Mr T. W. French, Dr E. A. Gee, Mr J. Ingamells, Dr D. M. Palliser, Messrs H. G. Ramm, Maurice Smith, and J. E. Williams.

While it is impossible to thank individually all of those who have signally helped me in research, I must pay tribute to the efficiency and the generous assistance of many institutions, notably the York City Library, the City Art Gallery, the Minster Library, the Borthwick Institute, and the library of the Institute of Advanced Architectural Studies. Outside York I have been likewise befriended by the Leeds City Library and its Archives Department, the Brotherton Library of Leeds University, and the library of the Yorkshire Archaeological Society; the Deeds Registries of the three Ridings and the County Record Offices at Beverley and Northallerton; several departments of the British Museum; the Public Record Office; and the Bodleian Library, Oxford. My work has benefited greatly from the ability to borrow books from the London Library and the library of the Society of Antiquaries. For the use of graphic and photographic material I am obliged to the National Monuments Record and to the libraries of the Royal Institute of British Architects and the Victoria and Albert Museum.

The book owes much to my publishers, especially to Sam Carr who suggested it, and has watched over it throughout; to Douglas Sellick; and to Celia Hollis. The chief contributor at all stages has been my wife who, in addition, has read the proofs.

John H. Harvey
January 1974

Introduction

The coloured view of the towers of the Minster over Bootham Bar, advertising Rowntrees' York Chocolate on a calendar, hung on the wall of the little stone shop in Bethlehem. When he was not calling up to his wife, who kept hens on the roof, to ask if there were eggs – *Miriam, fi baid?* – the Christian Arab grocer would expatiate, through linguistic barriers, on his pride and pleasure at living under the mandatory government of Britain. The year was 1934, the British Empire still flourished, symbolised by a calendar depicting historic York. It was as though York were Bethlehem's elder brother, verifying the old saw that 'Durham is old and York was when King David ruled Jerusalem'. The facts are different: Bethlehem already existed, on the documentary evidence of the Amarna tablets, by 1400 BC: *Bit ilu Lahmu*, sanctuary of the god of Corn or of the goddess Lahama, 400 years before David's time. York, unusual among great cities, is a modern foundation of known date, AD 71, some five centuries younger than even *the* New City, Neapolis or Naples.

There was, however, a real link between ancient Palestine and the founding of *Eboracum* in northern Britain. The consolidation of the Roman Empire under Vespasian demanded first the subjugation of unruly Palestine, concluded with the capture of Jerusalem in the late summer of AD 70. It is no mere coincidence, but cause and effect, that this made possible a controlled expansion on the opposite, north-western frontier, in the next year. The province of Britain, after the invasion of Claudius in AD 43, extended effectively only as far as the Fosse Way, slanting from Lincoln down to Bath. To the north lay the tributary kingdom of the Brigantes, covering most of England beyond Trent. It remains an open question whether that nation had any capital city and, if so, whether it lay at or near the site of the new Roman station. Some have believed in a Brigantian capital on the site of York, others that it was at Aldborough.

According to the legendary British History as perpetuated by Geoffrey of Monmouth, the city of Ebrauc, 'Kaerebrauc', was founded by king Ebraucus son of Mempricius about the time that King David reigned in Judaea (i.e. traditionally *c.* 1000 BC). Later events said to have occurred at York were a great council held by king Belinus about 390 BC, after his conquest of Denmark; and about 300 BC the coronation of Arthgallo by his brother Elidur. King Cassivelaunus, who had historical existence as the opponent of Julius Caesar in 54 BC, was said to have been buried at York six years later. We need not follow the legendary account of the coming of Christianity to York and the local aspects of the Arthurian period, but there may be some truth in Geoffrey's account of the conversion of pagan archflamens and flamens into the Christian archbishops and bishops of Britain. The three seats of the archflamens were in London, York, and Caerleon, and Eborius, bishop of York, actually did attend the Council of Arles in AD 314.

The names Ebrauc, Eboracum, and Eborius lead to a consideration of the etymology of York. The subject is extremely difficult because of the remarkable coincidences with which it is beset. The earliest form, in the Greek of the geographer Ptolemy, is Eborakon, corresponding to the usual Latin Eboracum. For a start, this is identical with *Ebora*, now Evora in Portugal, and it is reasonable to think that the same basic meaning should underlie the names of both cities. The philological experts tell us that the root is that of a British word *eburos*, a yew tree: either the city was named from an abundance of yews, or from a person bearing the name which, in slightly altered form, was that of the bishop of 314. It is not inconceivable, then, that the legend of Ebrauc may be fundamentally true, and the place named after him. On the other hand, the later versions, from the tenth to the fifteenth century, centre around Euerwic or Euerwich, apparently meaning the (commercial or harbour) district or suburb (*wic*, *wich*) on the river Ure; or alternatively a double name for the twin towns on opposite banks of the river. In this case Ebor(acum) and Wic would be exactly comparable to Maastricht and Wijk, its trading port across the bridge; or to Buda and Pest. In any case a direct derivation from yew trees must be ruled out. Situation and soil are unfavourable, and the yew is conspicuous by its absence (as a wild tree) from almost the whole of York-shire.

The geographical position of York underlies its historical importance. Although York is 40 or 50 miles from the open sea, the river has always been navigable up to the city by sea-going vessels and, until the making of Naburn Lock in 1757, the tides went some ten miles further up, beyond the confluence of the Nidd. The site of York is the outcome of the two factors: the upper limit of navigation for large vessels; and the lowest point where the river could be forded, or easily bridged. The ford was due to the crossing of the Vale by a glacial moraine, a ridge running from east to west and just high enough to provide an early trade route which ran across the 'neck' of England as part of through communications from the Continent to Ireland. The confluence with the Ouse of the river Foss and its tributaries lies just to the north of the ridge, and the peninsula between the two rivers provides an easily defensible area of high land.

It was this defensible spot that caught the skilled eye of the Roman governor Petilius Cerialis when he sought to occupy the Brigantian territory. The late Sir Ian Richmond well remarked that by this choice 'Roman initiative once and for all determined the position of the Northern Command in England'. This fundamentally strategic value has to be emphasised, for what was made in AD 71 was not a city but a fortress pure and simple, designed for the occupation of the Ninth Legion under the command of Cerialis ten years earlier and now picked by him to pioneer the advance into northern Britain. The growth of a civilian settlement between the fortress and the left bank of the river, and of a chartered town opposite, was secondary. The *canabae* or booths, close to the wall of the fortress, were granted on short leases to tradesmen who catered for the needs of the garrison. The separate town to the south-west of the Ouse, on the contrary, had honorific rank as a *colonia*, wholly distinct from the military settlement, and before AD 213 had become the capital of Britannia Inferior, roughly the equivalent to England north of Trent. The seal was set upon the pre-eminent standing of Eboracum when it was chosen as the seat of the Imperial Court under Severus and Caracalla, and a palace was built early in the 3rd century.

Though the site of this palace is unknown, it is at least a plausible hypothesis that it may have been in the north-western sector of the *colonia*, the site of the Old Railway Station. This had certainly been the area of the mediaeval royal palace before 1227, when Henry III granted it to the Dominican Friars. In the Roman palace on 4 February 211 died Septimius Severus, by origin a Punic-speaking African born at Leptis Magna and thus the first Roman Emperor to have learned Latin as a foreign tongue. By his death his eldest son Caracalla – by some suspected of hastening his father's end – became Emperor at York. Almost a century later, in June 306, another Emperor, Constantius Chlorus died there, but the supposed birth of his son, later Constantine the Great, in York in 288 is apocryphal. Soon after his father's death he was proclaimed Augustus by the troops in York, but it was not until 324 that he became Emperor himself. The last of the Emperors to stay in York was probably Constans, son of Constantine, during his northern campaign of 343.

In spite of the official distinction awarded to the Roman settlement, which in the later Empire became also the residence of a civil governor, the general level of its architectural remains is poor. Few artists of quality can have been attracted to the place, and even the great columns of the Roman headquarters building in the fortress, discovered beneath the Minster, are clumsy in the extreme. Hardly any of the small objects found are of notable beauty or of outstanding technical quality. By far the most distinguished single item is also one of the most important from a strictly historical viewpoint: the magnificent fragment of an inscription from a tablet of AD 108. This records the building under the Emperor Trajan of the south-eastern gateway of the fortress by the Ninth Legion. This legion was very soon afterwards to disappear from history, probably in disgrace, and its place was henceforth taken in York by the Sixth, possibly at the beginning of the governorship of Platorius Nepos in 122. The great inscription of 108 rivals that of Trajan's column in Rome and that of the splendid memorial to the procurator Classicianus found in London on Tower Hill. All must have been set out in brush-strokes by artists of genius, very likely Greeks by origin, so markedly does the inspiration of their work excel the usual Roman standards.

The remains of mosaic pavements, of good but not of superlative quality, must also be attributed to travelling craftsmen provided with sound pattern-books. Of all the remains of Roman York, however, that which attracts most attention is the Multangular Tower. This was added to the western angle of the fortress in the 4th century, perhaps under Constantius I shortly before his death. The masonry of small blocks is of sound type and the scale of the surviving fragment is impressive. If anything may stand as a symbol of the Roman epoch in York it is this defensive tower, added to the fortress at a time when the storm clouds began to gather. A hundred years later and the legion was leaving for ever, though in 428 the Sixth Legion was still stationed at Eboracum according to the nominal record of the Notitia Dignitatum. Known as *Victrix*, the victorious, it is fitting that the name of this body of disciplined men should thus survive the general withdrawal which, as far as this country was concerned, was the end of the Roman Empire.

The human social history of Roman York has left many traces. There is ample evidence of one important local industry, the manufacture of ornaments from Whitby jet, carried out on the site of the Railway Station, outside the wall of the *colonia*. Blocks in the rough, partly shaped for making pins, which were turned after the heads had been cut, were found, implying a workshop, while many finished objects, including carved pendants, came from the graves of a later cemetery in the same area, dating from the 3rd and 4th centuries. There is not much evidence of other manufactured goods, though it seems not unlikely that the North was exporting cloaks (*tossia*) perhaps made of fur. Clay tiles and finials must have been made in the neighbourhood, many of them stamped for the Sixth Legion: one roofing tile bears the inscription, scribbled by the maker's finger: 'Pollio to the guild, good luck!' (*Polio colegio felictr*). Amulets and votive objects, as well as altars, are found dedicated to many and various gods of the pagan world. The stone leg from a votive table bears two inscriptions in Greek, by one Scribonius Demetrius, dedicating it to the gods of the governor's residence, and to Ocean and Tethys, his consort, who presided over the furthest ends of the world. This unusual detail has enabled the donor to be identified with an historical schoolmaster Demetrius who in AD 84 at Delphi in

ROMAN ROADS TO YORK

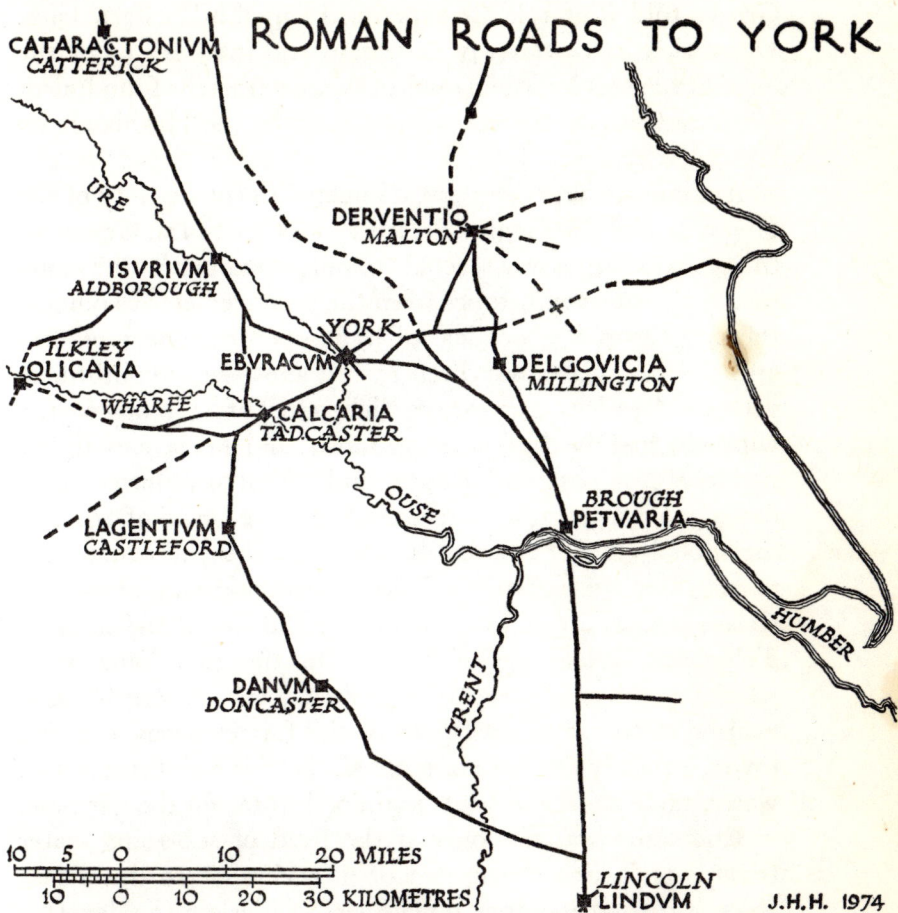

CATARACTONIVM
CATTERICK

URE

ISVRIVM
ALDBOROUGH

ILKLEY
OLICANA

DERVENTIO
MALTON

YORK
EBVRACVM

WHARFE

CALCARIA
TADCASTER

DELGOVICIA
MILLINGTON

OUSE

LAGENTIVM
CASTLEFORD

BROUGH
PETVARIA

HUMBER

DANVM
DONCASTER

TRENT

| 10 | 5 | 0 | 10 | 20 MILES |
| 10 | 0 | 10 | 20 | 30 KILOMETRES |

LINCOLN
LINDVM

J.H.H. 1974

York at the centre of a system of Roman roads. The city lies between two
main routes from Lincoln to the North and was served by transverse
linking roads. This explains many of the peculiarities of its later plan.

Greece told Plutarch his experiences in the Western Isles. Demetrius had evidently served in the intelligence of the expedition which pushed on northwards after the founding of York and carried the occupation as far as the Highlands by about the year 80.

Among the altars one was dedicated to the divinity of the Emperor and the Genius of York; another to the Genius of the place; a statue was erected 'to holy Britannia'. The many inscriptions on tombstones from the great cemeteries outside the city throw a good deal of light upon legionary officers and other officials, and often record ages, sadly youthful: a veteran of 43 with 23 years service; a girl of 13, a boy of 3; a wife who had lived 39 years 7 months and 11 days, with her children of 1 year and 3 days, and 1 year 9 months and 5 days; 31, 3, 13, 27; a centurion of 38, a decurion of 29. The melancholy tale continues. It is a more cheerful occupation to consider the remains of the Roman harbour along the river Foss, whose old course ran by the site of the modern Telephone Exchange of 1952. On the east bank were wharves and at the top of the west bank, where it came nearest to the south-east gate of the fortress, was a strong tower, possibly the base of a crane. To this point, then tidal water, came ships and boats to unload stores for the garrison.

Eboracum was not only at the head of sea-going water transport; it was the centre of a system of roads. These Roman roads have, for 19 centuries, underlain the developing pattern of the historic city. Their actual placing on the ground had, and to this day has, the highest significance. A great deal that puzzles the visitor makes sense only when the early layout is studied on the map (p. 7). Accustomed in modern times to think in terms of 'North at the top', and of York as roughly half-way on a notional meridian between London and Edinburgh (which, incidentally, lies 120 miles west of London as well as 300 miles north), the street pattern of York and the lines of approach are mystifying. York is not

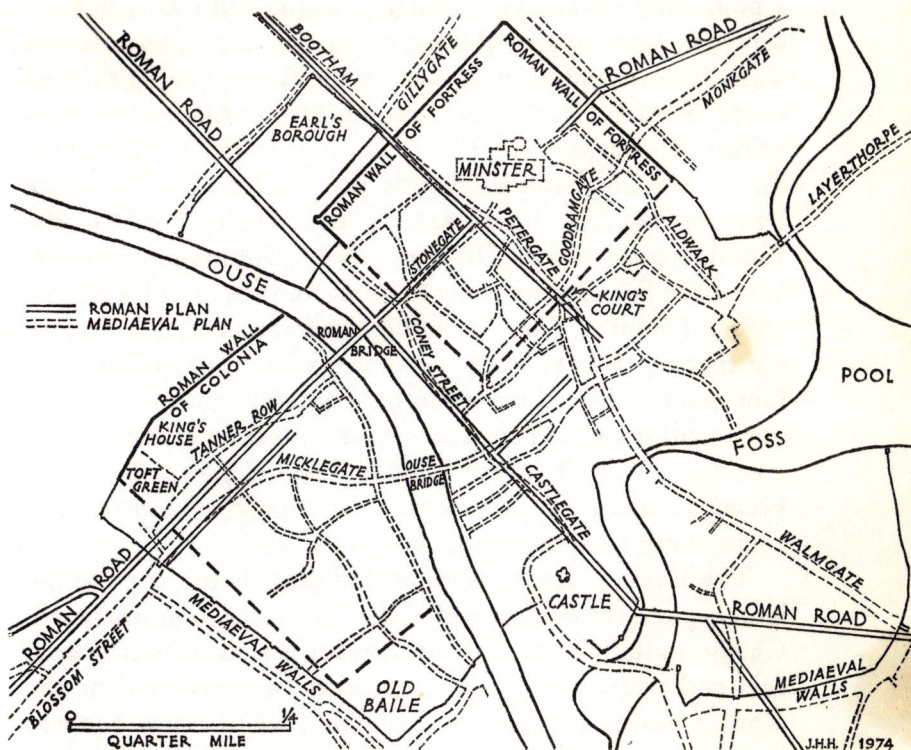

Key:
- ═══ ROMAN PLAN
- ┅┅┅ MEDIAEVAL PLAN

Map labels: ROMAN ROAD, BOOTHAM, GILLYGATE, ROMAN WALL OF FORTRESS, ROMAN ROAD, MONKGATE, EARL'S BOROUGH, MINSTER, ROMAN WALL OF FORTRESS, LAYERTHORPE, ALDWARK, OUSE, STONEGATE, PETERGATE, GOODRAMGATE, KING'S COURT, POOL, ROMAN WALL OF COLONIA, ROMAN BRIDGE, CONEY STREET, KING'S HOUSE, TANNER ROW, TOFT GREEN, MICKLEGATE, OUSE BRIDGE, CASTLEGATE, FOSS, ROMAN ROAD, WALMGATE, CASTLE, ROMAN ROAD, BLOSSOM STREET, MEDIAEVAL WALLS, OLD BAILE, MEDIAEVAL WALLS, QUARTER MILE, J.H.H. 1974

Mediaeval York superimposed on the Roman fortress, to the north-east of the Ouse, and the civil *colonia* opposite. The city incorporated both, together with suburban commercial districts, and the port to the south and east. The new pattern of streets is largely based on the crossing of the river at Ouse Bridge and consequent deflection from the Roman alignment.

a point on an even approximately north–south axis, but the centre of a crossing of oblique roads running rather east and west. It lies about 12 miles east of the A1, following the line of the Roman North Road from Lincoln (*Lindum*) to Corbridge (*Corstopitum*) on the Wall and beyond. In the other direction a road ran eastwards to connect with the route between Brough (*Petuaria*) on the north shore of the Humber and Malton (*Derventio*). Traces of branching roads have been found, short cuts to north and south of this cross-axis on the map. Turning to the detailed plan of the city, we see that the Roman plan was not cardinal but ordinal: the four walls of the legionary fortress faced north-west, north-east, south-east, and south-west, and its main axis ran from a bridge on the site of the Guildhall and along the line of St Helen's Square and Stonegate, beneath the Minster and again along Chapter House Street (p. 9).

The Roman layout corresponded directly to the lie of the land beyond the bridgehead of the Tadcaster (*Calcaria*) road. Changes after the end of the Roman period have obscured this and made the old arrangements nonsensical. For the Roman bridge was broken down and, when a new one was built, it was nearly a quarter-mile downstream and crossed the river almost due east and west. The approach roads bypassed the fortress and, as bypasses usually are, were curving rather than straight. Traffic from the south to the north, touching York, has always moved through a right-angle, coming from Tadcaster to the south-west, and leaving York by Bootham Bar, facing north-west towards Edinburgh. Even though, schematically, this change of direction has always been dictated by the Roman plan, its details have been altered in the course of time. Hardly any of the roads and streets lie precisely upon their Roman predecessors, but rather sidle alongside or meander across like variations on a theme. Finally comes a majestic, crashing discord: the Minster, as we shall see later, was deliberately planted on a true east–west alignment about 1080 by the first Norman archbishop, Thomas of Bayeux.

We cannot doubt that the placing of the Minster on a new site and with true orientation was intended as a defiance of the pagan traditions that had hitherto ruled the city. But the Minster stands almost alone: most of the parish churches face north-east, following the Roman direction or diverging slightly from it; one, St Michael-le-Belfrey beside the Minster, points to the south-east beside Petergate, successor to the Via Principalis. This diversity of orientation, along with the confusing web of streets and lanes laid out at different dates, gives to the whole city a cock-eyed look and an unexpectedness that render it unique. There is no such thing in York as a direct approach, head-on, except to the four great stone gateways of the Bars. Every other viewpoint is sidelong, glancing, accidental. The effect is heightened by the course of the Ouse, wandering about so that it seems unable to make up its mind whether it is flowing to the east or to the south, and doing both.

The offbeat genius of the place – the god to whom an early citizen dedicated an altar found at the Railway Station, '*Deo genio loci*' – saw to it that even altogether new means of transport should not avoid the traditional kink. When a railway from London to York was first contemplated, the corporation of the city agreed that lands at Tang Hall, east of York, should be made available. Such a line would have come from due south, passing the city on the north-east on its way to Newcastle and Edinburgh. The station might have been somewhere near Layerthorpe. It seemed otherwise to the presiding genius, and the route chosen, though not precisely that taken by the old Tadcaster Road, was also from the same general direction, and ran parallel to the road for the last two miles, reaching the western corner of the walled area near Micklegate Bar. For no known reason it was determined that the station must be actually within the

walls, and a great arch was cut. The line penetrated the city
and its terminus was built on the site of the ancient royal
palace, later Dominican Friary, and more recent York
Nursery gardens. This dead end meant that, by the time the
station was opened, two railways entered it from south and
north and all through trains had to reverse. Within five years
a branch to Scarborough had been added, so arranged that
a through train from London would have to reverse twice!

Yet this apparent curse produced by indirection one of
York's greatest blessings and noblest creations, the new
Railway Station designed by Thomas Prosser in 1867 and
opened ten years later. When built, York Station was the
largest in the world; it is still one of the most impressive, its
finest feature being the majestic curve of its plan. This was
forced upon it by the need to arrange the lines for through
running from south to north and west to east: London to
Scotland and Leeds to Scarborough. The new station did not
merely cancel out the fundamental error of the old: its main
entrance, and exit, facing a high section of the city rampart
and walls, brings the arriving traveller face to face with
York as soon as he leaves the train. There can be few more
impressive confrontations than this, particularly in spring
when the whole rampart is clad with thousands of daffodils
in full bloom. Swords are beaten into ploughshares and
ramparts become fields of asphodel.

The more distant approach, at any rate from the south, is
not impressive by rail, for the line runs in a shallow cutting
and the skyline of the city is not visible. From the North,
however, there is a splendid series of views of the Minster
and city from the north-west and from due west, with the
river in front. The main roads still provide a closer view of
the bars, though one-way street systems in most cases prevent
the traveller from entering, unless in a small vehicle or on
foot. By far the finest route is that by the old main road from
Tadcaster, passing the green spaces of the Knavesmire with

the racecourse and climbing to the top of The Mount, from which a broad gentle slope, lined with cobblestones and trees, leads down to Micklegate Bar and the 'Great Street' (Mickla gata) of mediaeval York. By this road we pass Copmanthorpe, the settlement of the merchants, perhaps the point at a safe distance outside the gates where foreigners could be lodged or kept in quarantine. Like the streets in the city, the mediaeval and modern highroad swings and sways from side to side of the Roman alignment, touched here and there but mostly abandoned.

The reason for the dereliction of the old roads and streets was that they became impassable. Inside the built-up area this was probably due mainly to the ruin and collapse of the houses along the frontages: the streets were blocked, and it was simpler to clear a new line behind the ruined houses on one side or the other. Across the countryside the roads, for lack of mending, fell into potholes and seas of mud. Again, it was the easiest course to form a new causeway clear of the churned-up morass cluttered with blocks of stone from the old paving. Lanes and footpaths preserve the line of The Old Street for most of the way to Tadcaster, but inside York the Roman streets are ghosts of the back yards. In the suburbs, where they were lined with tombs, houses stand on the ancient graveyard and quiet gardens cover the metalling trodden by the legionaries.

It is customary to think of the collapse of Roman rule in Britain, and the onset of the Dark Age, as more or less simultaneous. Within roughly one generation, we used to be told, civilisation broke down and invading pagans from the continent, Saxons, Angles, and others, made a clean sweep and built another world of rural villages. There is indeed some truth in this picture, demonstrated by the complete abandonment of many Roman towns: Verulamium, supplanted by St Alban's; Venta, removed to Norwich. Shrewsbury was substituted for Viroconium, Southampton for Clausentum, Hull for Petuaria; Calleva (Silchester) was deserted. On the other hand, it is certain that there was some real continuity in the history of London, and in spite of ruin and rebuilding there was continuity of site at least in many cases, among them Canterbury, Colchester, Exeter, Gloucester, Leicester, Lincoln, Winchester, and York. What really happened?

It begins to look as though there is more fundamental truth in the Welsh chronicles and in the 'British History' than used to be admitted. The Romans did not sweep away wholesale the British kingdoms and principalities, which in some cases must have preserved their traditions outside the formal jurisdiction of the military fortresses and civil governorates set up by Rome. The withdrawal of the legions certainly did not mean a complete simultaneous cessation of civil government, and civilised and educated Britons and British princes were undoubtedly able to take over in some places. There is every likelihood that this was the case at York. Not just life went on, but for a time an ordered life with the same streets, houses, shops, and public buildings, ships tying up at the same quays along the Foss and Ouse. It was not until AD 446 that the famous letter was sent, by the official British government be it noted, to the general Aetius. Aetius, an authentic historical personage, was the last successful Roman leader in the West, and he might indeed have been able to listen to 'the groans of the Britons' and press back the barbarian raiders of whom they complained. As it was, he won near Châlons-sur-Marne on 20 September 451 the great victory over Attila and his Huns that changed the course of European history.

Aetius did not send help, and somehow Britain had to accommodate herself to slowly worsening conditions. It was perhaps no mere coincidence that, in 447, the year after the appeal to Aetius, St Germanus of Auxerre visited Britain and found Christian congregations still living an organised life.

The evidence from burials of the 4th century shows that York did not become suddenly and entirely converted to the new religion. A new fashion of burial in gypsum was largely followed, but by residual pagans as well as by Christians. It was not until 392 that pagan temples were finally closed throughout the Empire by the Edict of Theodosius, so that a great revolution in religious and social thought was still in progress at the time that direct Roman administration came to an end. As far back as the end of the 3rd century there had been settlement of continental Teutonic auxiliaries around Eboracum, and this local association undoubtedly paved the way for the employment of Saxons as mercenary protectors of the British community when the final appeal to Aetius produced no help. By about 450 Roman Eboracum had given place to British Caer Ebrauc living in uneasy companionship with bands of Germanic speakers who, it may be supposed, were paid by grants of land around York.

It was at this point that a major natural disaster supervened to put an end to the old city. Great floods, which can be dated archaeologically to the century between 450 and 550, overwhelmed all the lower parts of York to a depth of 35 feet above sea level (Ordnance Datum). This catastrophe destroyed the Roman bridge and the wharves and quays of the river port. So far as York and its region are concerned, we need seek no further for the main cause of the break between the Roman city and its successor. Several feet of mud and silt over a great part of the inhabited area, notably the commercial districts, give an unmistakable answer. There is every likelihood that it was as a result of the great flood that York ceased to have the status of a capital, a British dynasty withdrawing westwards to Sherburn and thence ruling the kingdom of Elmet until Cerdic, last of his line, was driven out by Edwin early in the 7th century.

The mysterious British kingdom of Elmet also provides an answer to the fragmentation of the Anglo-Saxon

settlement of northern England. It formed a wedge of still un-
conquered territory, in touch with Chester and North Wales,
and stretching eastwards to the lower valleys of the rivers
Aire, Wharfe, and Ouse. Beyond its existence and the name
of its last king, very little is known of Elmet, but as *Elmed
saetna* it comprised 600 hides of land, an area nearly equal
to the later Yorkshire wapentakes of Skyrack and Barkston
Ash. The latter was the meeting place of the wapentake, an
ash tree in the township of Barkston and parish of Sherburn.
Skyrack, understood to mean 'the shire oak', or oak tree at
which the men of the region assembled, also included places
described as 'in Elmet', as well as Leeds and a number of
other parishes associated with it in the early district called
Loidis. Since the group of 'Leeds' parishes was mostly
within Elmet, it is assumed that Loidis and Elmet together
formed a single kingdom. Two historical facts tend to con-
firm this, and to link Elmet directly with York. The first is
the subdivision of the mediaeval archdeaconry of York into
deaneries, two of which were Old Ainsty and New Ainsty.
Together these covered the whole area of Loidis and Elmet,
as well as the wapentake of Ainsty always closely associated
with the city (p. 17).

It is well established that ancient church boundaries tend
to represent an earlier state of affairs than those of civil
administration. In this case, the limits of the deaneries are
probably older than those of the wapentakes. This in turn
links with the second piece of evidence, connecting Elmet
with the history of York. Within the area of Elmet a very
substantial amount of land belonged to the archbishop and
church of York, and notably the whole parishes of Sherburn-
in-Elmet and Otley. The archbishop had very ancient
palaces at both places, and that at Sherburn was the head of
a barony belonging to him throughout the Middle Ages. The
archbishop's important palace next to York Minster and
all his other property in and around the city formed

KINGDOM OF ELMET

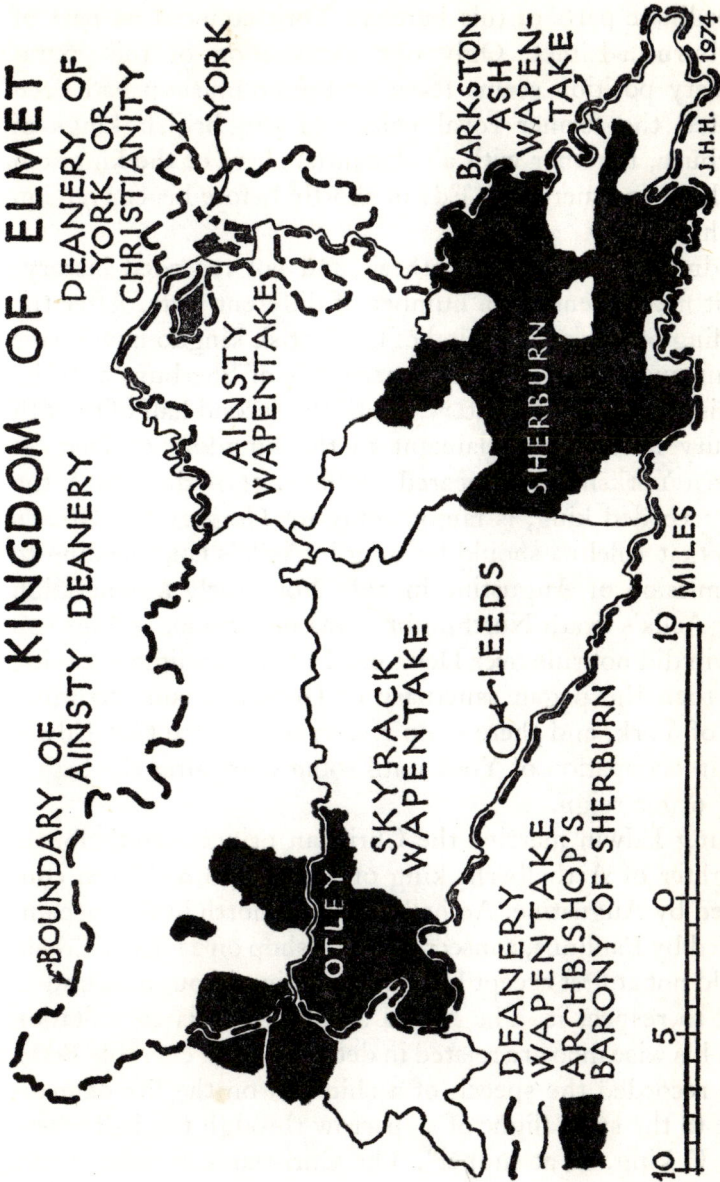

DEANERY OF YORK OR CHRISTIANITY

BOUNDARY OF AINSTY DEANERY

YORK

AINSTY WAPENTAKE

BARKSTON ASH WAPENTAKE

SHERBURN

SKYRACK WAPENTAKE

OTLEY

LEEDS

J.H.H. 1974

DEANERY
WAPENTAKE
ARCHBISHOP'S BARONY OF SHERBURN

10   5   0   10 MILES

The ancient rural deanery of Ainsty, which included and possibly represented the British kingdom of Loidis (Leeds) and Elmet. The lands given to the archbishop and forming his barony of Sherburn may have been the earlier royal domain of Cerdic, last British king of Elmet.

subordinate parts of this barony: York counted as part of Sherburn-in-Elmet. Only one explanation of this extraordinary position seems feasible: the archbishop had been granted the former royal palace of the British kings at Sherburn, together with a substantial share of the kingdom of Elmet conquered by Edwin shortly before his conversion to Christianity.

Admittedly this is hypothesis and not recorded history; but it makes sense of a number of different facts. After the flooding of York the capital of the British kingdom will have been transferred to the little acropolis of Sherburn with its unmistakable air of mastery. Until the second half of the 6th century no Anglian claimant to the kingdom of Deira – eastern Yorkshire – appeared. Aella (*c.* 560– died 588), the first recorded king, is famous only for Gregory the Great's pun, that Alleluia should be sung in Aella's land, leading to the mission of Augustine in 596. For nearly a generation after Aella's death Northumbria was in turmoil, and his son Edwin did not rule over Deira until 616. Its religious capital was then the pagan sanctuary of Goodmanham, 20 miles east of York, and there is no reason to suppose that Edwin was in occupation of York until some years after the beginning of his reign.

King Edwin married the Christian princess Aethelburh, daughter of Aethelberht king of Kent, who had been converted by Augustine. Aethelburh came north in 625 accompanied by Paulinus, consecrated as bishop on 21 July. Edwin would not at first accept his wife's religion, though he undertook to respect it. The king's doubts and his consultation with his wise men are related in detail by the Venerable Bede, who recorded the speech of a chieftain on the life of man: 'like to the swift flight of a sparrow through the hall where you, O king, sit at supper'. The Christian certainty as to a future life won the day, the high priest Coifi set fire to the temple at Goodmanham, and on 12 April 627 Edwin was baptised in a wooden church at York which he had had built for the purpose while he was receiving instruction from Paulinus. Soon afterwards he caused a larger church to be built of stone, surrounding the timber chapel. This first Saxon church at York was dedicated to St Peter and is regarded as the original York Minster, though it now appears to have stood on a different site.

Nothing of Edwin's cathedral has been discovered, but within the last five years another stone building of the period has been found in York. This is a tower filling a gap in the partly destroyed Roman wall on the north-west side of the fortress. So far as any parallel can be produced for its type of construction, it is the western porch of the Northumbrian church at Monkwearmouth, built late in the 7th century. It seems likely that Edwin, after occupying York but before his final defeat of Cerdic, strengthened the defences against attacks by the British of Elmet. Some confirmation of this comes from Welsh poems of the period, which refer to Elmet, to the harassing of York, and to a muster for the burning of York. The masonry of the York tower implies a distant influence from Rome, greatly diluted, and may well be due to craftsmen brought by Paulinus from Kent. Whatever its origin, the Anglian Tower is unique, and provides a glimmer of light in the Dark Age.

The reign of King Edwin and his conversion to Christianity mark the beginning of York, superseding Eboracum which, though partly destroyed by the floods, stood on the site. Archaeological excavations in the last few years, notably those beneath the Minster, have shown that not only in the 7th century, but much later, there must have been extensive remains of the Roman buildings of the fortress and the civil city. In spite of the decay due to lack of maintenance and the end – in the 5th century – of Roman methods of central heating, the new inhabitants must have been able to make use of a good deal. It is probable, though not certain, that the new church of St Peter was placed within the head-quarters building of the fortress, and this was very likely taken by Edwin as his palace. Whatever Anglo-Saxon repugnance he may have felt to living in the large stone buildings of a city would have been overcome by his contact with Paulinus, fresh from Rome and Gaul.

The glimmer of civilisation under Edwin was soon put out by civil war and a renewal of paganism. Paulinus became a fugitive, and for a long time little is known of York beyond the continuing occupation of its site. Even so the evidence is slight, and another 300 years were to go by before yielding any substantial art. Even then there are only fragments of carved stone crosses and tomb slabs, and York shines rather in its recorded history than in its archaeological remains. The great glory of early York was Alcuin, one of the few outstanding men of learning in a period still dim. Born in York *c.* 735 he was educated in the cathedral school which already existed, taught by Aelbert, who in 766 became archbishop, Alcuin succeeding him as master. Alcuin visited Rome with Aelbert to find manuscripts and between 780 and 790 served at the court of Charlemagne, where he was the effective founder of the Palace School. Returning to York in 790 he found conditions too bad to prolong his stay: 'What should I do in Northumbria where no one is free from fear?' So he went back to France and ended his days as abbot of St Martin at Tours in 804. Perhaps the earliest instance of the brain-drain from Britain produced by misgovernment, Alcuin carried Northumbrian culture outwards to a wider sphere. He made of Charlemagne's school at Aachen in the years 782–96 the first effective university in north-western Europe. Alcuin himself recorded his debt to his native city, with its walls and towers and its trade by sea and land. Europe acknowledges the leadership of Alcuin in the Carolingian Renaissance, the first light of a new dawn. Alcuin reflected the glory back upon his beloved birthplace York.

1 A View of York Today

York means many things to many people, but in the last few years three topics have overwhelmed all others: the University, the Minster, and Conservation. Residents are constantly plied with questions from their outside acquaintance upon these subjects, and they are clearly matters of outstanding public interest and concern. For it must be remembered, even though normally forgotten by the York citizens themselves, that York's image to the outside world is pre-eminently that of a *historic* city. York's fate as a collective monument of historic and architectural interest is a matter of primary national concern: it is the English Toledo or even Venice. Hence the interest in conservation, often carried to a point which born Yorkers regard as exaggerated and intrusive; but which they must come to accept as natural and inevitable. The continued existence, not simply of York as a going concern, but recognisably as the sum total of a great past, is vital.

The Minster, as the greatest single building in York and as the church which epitomises the spiritual history of the city, towers over the general issue of conservation as it does over the houses. In the public mind it ranks next after the greatest monuments of London and Westminster as living history. The news, in 1967, that a sum of two million pounds sterling was being asked for to forestall collapse, focused attention upon it, and interest was maintained by the unexpected opportunity afforded for thorough archaeological investigation. Nowhere else, except at Winchester in the few preceding years, had a major cathedral site been excavated. And whereas at Winchester the site of the early cathedral was identified outside the existing fabric (as indeed by exclusion seems also to be true at York), it was beneath the present Minster that archaeologists dug and studied for some seven years on end. Even though the Saxon cathedral has not yet been discovered, the finds are of immense artistic and historical importance.

The University, though less exciting as 'hot news', has seized upon the national imagination to a surprising degree, and this in spite of the fact that its site is not actually in York, though it is now (1975) in the same new county of North Yorkshire. The belated acquisition of a university is certainly a strange phenomenon here. Considering the importance of the old cathedral school under Aelbert and Alcuin as far back as the 8th century – the nearest thing to a university in Europe and far earlier even than the Muslim universities of Fez (860) and Cairo – it is amazing that York did not attain academic status until more than four centuries after the end of the Middle Ages. All the crop of 'red-brick' universities sprang up first, and several of the concrete-and-glass swarm, before York achieved its ancient ambition. The reasons are not easy to grasp, but among them the sheer indifference of the South for the North is prominent.

It is this factor in English historical development, parallel to the converse phenomenon in France and Spain, which has in the past loaded York's shoulder with a heavy chip. With hardly any exceptions since the reign of Richard II in the fourteenth century, the North in general and its capital

York in particular, have felt neglected. In many ways they really have been overlooked, and the neglect is more automatic and less spiteful than tends to be assumed. So far as the university is concerned, the obvious initial reason for its failure to materialise is that given by Alcuin. Northumbria fell apart politically and was then taken over by barbarian Vikings for nearly a century. York did not share in the southern renaissance under king Alfred nor even in the relatively peaceful development of Saxon and Dane together that marked eastern England after the treaty of Wedmore. The last hundred years up to and beyond the Norman Conquest were again destructive rather than constructive. It was not until late in the twelfth century that the city once more became a cultural centre.

Notwithstanding the remarkable spread of the idea of universities in the twelfth century, with the real (as opposed to the traditional) founding of Oxford, the total number in Europe remained small for several hundred years. It has to be borne in mind that the small country of England had acquired two universities long before certain important nations had even one. Some Spanish universities were founded in the thirteenth century, and so was Prague, but not one was opened until the fourteenth in Portugal, Poland, or Hungary. In Scotland St Andrews was not founded until 1411, followed by Glasgow in 1453 and Aberdeen in 1494. Renewed pressure, after the end of the Middle Ages, came from the Protestant reformers principally, though Henry viii had the intention of founding a college at Durham, and this project was repeated under the Commonwealth. It was at the same time that a petition was put forward for the founding of a university at York, to be financed out of the confiscated revenues of the Church. Nothing happened, and it was Durham that – first after Oxford and Cambridge – eventually got its university in 1832, though its charter was not granted until 1837, a year later than that for London.

This promotion of Durham, always a rival, came as a bitter blow to York.

That York did in our own time achieve its long-term ambition is due mainly to the determination of the late John Bowes Morrell, twice Lord Mayor. Around him gathered a body of opinion which, soon after the end of the war of 1939–45, crystallised into a formal committee. Two academic institutes, deliberately intended to form integral parts of a future university, were founded and became effective in 1953: the Borthwick Institute for the study of archives, and the Institute of Advanced Architectural Studies. By 1960 official approval was obtained, work went ahead, and the university with its first two colleges opened to students in October 1963. In more than one respect the fulfilment has accorded less with the ambitious dream than with the quirkish fantasy of the Genius Loci. The site found, the estate of Heslington Hall, lay outside the city boundaries, and to some citizens the gap between the imagined York University and the achieved 'university of Heslington' has seemed to be more than the physical three miles. The chosen plan of an open campus, with colleges and lecture rooms, central hall and library, spread over a very wide area, appears wasteful both in space and time, though the magnificent landscaping (by the late Frank Clark) of a fine existing estate is an acknowledged masterpiece. Another curious feature was the decision that Latin should not be a main subject, considering that the Borthwick Institute exists largely for the study of (Latin) ecclesiastical documents, and the university includes an important centre of mediaeval studies, in history and in fine arts . . .

In addition to the two pre-existing institutes, the university obtained the long lease of the splendid King's Manor in the city. This has become the new seat of the Institute of Architectural Studies with its select but important library, and also the Francis Wormald library for research in the

history of the fine arts. Two adjacent mansions in Micklegate, Bathurst House and Micklegate House opposite to
Holy Trinity church, were also acquired for teaching
purposes. Another important step was the arrangement
between the university and the cathedral chapter regarding
the Minster Library. This vital collection of ancient books
and manuscripts in cathedral premises is now staffed at
university expense and has been brought up to date. Though
the manuscripts of Alcuin's famous library were all destroyed or dispersed long ago, at least its tradition has
survived in this mediaeval library of the Minster, and forms
a direct link with the new university which, 1200 years later,
fulfils Alcuin's vision of learning. It is to be hoped that in
due course of time these footholds in the historic centre of
York will overcome the difficulties of physical separation.

Whereas the University exerts an intellectual sway, the
Minster dominates the scene by its physical presence. Ever
since the completion of its three towers in their present form
in 1472, the silhouette of the great church has loomed over
every distant view of the city and over a great many internal
glimpses. York without the Minster is now unthinkable,
and the mind boggles at the concept of Eboracum and of
Euerwich as they were. The startling idea that it might
actually fall down, even though felt to be heightened as a
fund-raising expedient, produced a wave of unprecedented
local patriotism. The impossible was achieved, but as usual
it took a little longer. In the process of raising the money a
good deal of serious harm was done to lesser objectives in the
same field, that of conservation. At the particular juncture of
1967, when the alarm was sounded, it was little short of a
tragedy that the very modest existing appeal for the modern-
isation of York Theatre Royal should have been over-
shadowed, and that the hopes of a fund to ensure the future
of the city's redundant churches were stifled. There can be
no doubt that buildings of national importance and on the

scale of the Minister should be maintained and repaired out of national funds. Competition with the claims of smaller monuments, however worthy, is disastrous.

It is to be supposed that the programme of repairs now completed will have ensured the physical safety of the fabric for a considerable time to come. So far so good. What is still better is that the archaeological work on the site has revealed the whole plan of the early Norman cathedral begun about 1080 by archbishop Thomas of Bayeux. Much of this was completely unexpected, not least the fact that it neither incorporated nor concealed any part of a Saxon church. Furthermore, a large area of late Saxon graveyard was found to have the tombs aligned to the Roman orientation of the headquarters building within whose limits it was placed. The Norman church was deliberately planted on a cleared site and set out on a fresh axis pointing with unusual accuracy to the true East. Substantial remains of the Roman buildings survived beneath the Norman foundations and included even large areas of painted wall plaster. The slight aesthetic interest of these remains is compensated for by their technical and historical significance. The Norman church was both outstanding in size and original in plan, with an unaisled nave of great span. The discovery explains one of the main puzzles of the existing cathedral: the enormous width of its nave between the present aisles. This was rebuilt in 1291 and later incorporated the mid-thirteenth century central tower, itself built on the Norman piers with additions; hence the present piers of the arcades stand on the stumps of the Norman outer walls.

A hundred years later than the Norman church were twin towers built outside its west front. This find gave the answer to another puzzle: why it was that the design of 1291 had been altered to provide for western towers not at first intended. It is now clear that the new Gothic nave was to have been built around the towers of the late twelfth century in the way that the Norman towers at Lincoln were preserved in the later screen, and as the old central tower at York was until its fall in 1407. Further evidence confirmed the historical record of a great fire in 1137, after which the Norman transepts were doubled in length, thus reaching the overall north–south dimension of the present Gothic church. Only to the east, in the Lady Chapel built in 1361–73, did the Gothic church go beyond the overall length of its predecessor, projecting into another parish and, in the end, causing the demolition of its church, St Mary ad Valvas, close against the new east front. It seems that even the narrow easternmost bay is explained as the result of having to clear the west end of St Mary, before a decision had been taken that it might be demolished.

Associated with the archaeological excavations were the investigations of two thirteenth-century tombs, of arch-bishops Walter de Gray (died 1255) and Godfrey de Ludham (died 1265). From these graves appeared remains of im-portant textiles, jewellery, and funeral plate, and that of Gray in particular was one of the very few graves of really high standing opened in this country under modern scientific conditions. Concurrent studies by the Royal Commission on Historical Monuments, already engaged on an inventory of the Minster, continue to bring to light much detail concern-ing all periods of the fabric, its enrichments and monuments. Within a few years it is likely that York Minster will have been published in greater and more comprehensive detail than any other English church. Another product of the repairs has been the formation of a central crypt, exposing to view some of the Roman and Norman remains in position, and also housing a museum and treasury.

From the specific case of the Minster we pass to the wider problem of conservation in York as a whole. This had already caused serious disquiet for some years before the appeal was launched on behalf of the Minster. Comparatively

slight damage was caused by enemy action in the war
of 1939–45, though the timberwork of the Guildhall was
burnt and the nearby church of St Martin-le-Grand in Coney
Street largely destroyed. After a long period of hesitation the
Guildhall was, rightly, re-roofed with a replica of the original
wooden piers and roof, hand-carved in oak. At St Martin's,
only the tower and the south aisle were preserved and re-
instated, with provision for the display of the fine stained
glass of the old west window, fortunately placed in safety
before the destruction of the fabric. Other buildings, not
damaged but derelict, were repaired and converted to new
uses: the disused church of St John, Micklegate, became the
Institute of Advanced Architectural Studies; the fifteenth-
century St Anthony's Hall was used for the Borthwick
Institute.

In an unobtrusive way a certain amount was being done
by owners of property to rehabilitate worthy old buildings in
the city, notably by the Ings Trust, but this only scratched
the surface of the problem of the streets and houses. Other
problems were steadily becoming more urgent, particularly
that of redevelopment within the walls and in the immediate
suburban area beyond them; and that of the very large
number of old parish churches, many of which were pastor-
ally redundant or likely soon to become so. The list of
buildings of special architectural or historic interest, prepared officially under the Town and Country Planning Act
of 1947, was one of the first to be made. Though this had
the advantage of calling attention soon after the war to the
importance of many outstanding York buildings, it suffered
from a corresponding disadvantage. The list was drawn up
before adequate experience had been gained of the legislation
required to give real protection, and before solutions had
been found to many of the questions of principle and of
practice that have had to be solved in the course of 25 years.

In the meantime two destructive forces were at work: the

demands of private developers for permission to pull down and rebuild, not only individual listed buildings, but whole blocks and areas of the city; and the wholesale programmes of clearance by the corporation, involving a great majority of the Victorian developments round York, before they had been considered for possible listing. These two threats were not entirely unconnected, in that there was a strong incentive to finance redevelopment by the local authority out of increased rateable value from new buildings put up for profit. A process of attrition began, and particularly within a few years after 1960 was making serious inroads upon the streetscape and the overall impression of York. To the negative threat, of piecemeal whittling away of the historic city, was added the positive threat of new blocks of buildings of over-powering scale and discordant design.

In spite of a spirit of enlightenment and much good will on the part of the staff of the planning office, and the existence in the area of several active amenity societies, a great deal of damage has been done. It has regretfully to be conceded that York is no longer what it was, even within very recent memory. This is not by any means simply a question of loss of valuable old buildings, notwithstanding their appearance on the official list as worthy of preservation. It is much more the sad fact that, in not a single case of replacement of an old building or block by a new one, is the modern building conceivably better than the old. It is true that in some few cases what was pulled down was already in poor physical condition, but even the sheer necessity of replacement does nothing to palliate the poverty of most of the new designs and their inexcusable lack of neighbourliness.

Two completely distinct faults have contributed to this regrettable result. On the one hand, English architectural design, with rare exceptions, has during the last quarter-century been at a low ebb. No amount of negative criticism, by architects' advisory panels or by anyone else, can infuse positive values into work that is simply bad or unsuitable. A right policy, for the country as a whole, might be to tighten controls and to make it far more difficult to secure permissions. In the end the present poverty of inspiration would cure itself, and encouragement could be given as better designs made their appearance. Secondly, proposals which involve the destruction of listed buildings ought not to be entertained at all unless certified by the relevant minister as required in the *national* interest. The listing is done impartially at national level; it should not be within the competence of local authorities to ask for buildings to be removed from the lists.

The other fault lies with planning committees, such as that in York, which fail to set an appropriate standard of scale, materials, and type of design for all buildings within a historic zone – what is now, or should be, designated as a conservation area. The worst damage to the townscape is done by excessive height: new buildings in positions where they can be visually associated with the old should not be allowed to rise above them, except for occasional towers or purely decorative features. In York there are several bad examples of undue height and bulk in the wrong place. In at least two cases, the Yorkshire Insurance building and the Viking Hotel, the designs are actually above the average, and the buildings would not be objectionable elsewhere. But the insurance block dwarfs the walls and is utterly out of keeping with its neighbours, and the hotel should never have been placed in close relation to one of the finest groups of mediaeval York: the church of All Saints, North Street, and the adjacent timbered houses.

Far worse than either of these buildings is the monstrous concrete brutality of the Stonebow development with its high-level car-park, looming above St Saviour's church. Especially as a part of the same planning improvement which had begun well with the brick telephone exchange, this is a tragedy. On the other hand, a much criticised concrete range of shops in Goodramgate, certainly unsuitable to the street, has at least been designed on the correct scale, and with a horizontality which rhymes with the older buildings. In such a case, where it is evident that a serious effort has been made, it is the character of the modern material that shows itself at fault. There is no possible compatibility between traditional materials: timber, plaster, brickwork, stone masonry, and the crudity of coarse concrete. Yet it is not concrete itself that is unsuitable. At the extension to the Theatre Royal, Mr Patrick Gwynne has shown what good design and sensitive handling of materials can do. The extension is of concrete and glass; but the concrete was hammer-dressed so that its surface is full of character, and is acceptable in close juxtaposition to the cleaned Victorian masonry of the old theatre and the brick and stucco of other neighbouring buildings.

In some cases the new buildings are simply anodyne rather than aggressive or objectionable; but they lack the positive qualities of what was destroyed to make way for them. One of the most regrettable instances of this is the new Prudential range on the north side of Blossom Street. The group of buildings destroyed had great charm and character and included two small brick houses of high quality, built in 1748–50, with infilling less distinguished but traditional and in character with the spacious feeling of the street. These buildings were in sound condition and should have been improved with the help of grants as a positive contribution to the main entry to the city. Not only their aesthetic qualities were of importance; the shops they housed were needed as part of the social amenities of the area, now lost. The same sad story is told in other parts of York, and there seems to be an evil genius which determines to sacrifice the best and most characteristic buildings in a given area. These are frequently public houses, and the recent losses of the Queen's

Head in Fossgate and the Plumbers' Arms in Skeldergate were quite pointless, examples of destruction for destruction's sake. Only serious outcry saved the Bay Horse and the Windmill, both in Blossom Street.

Another scandal is one that has no historical excuse in York of all places: the demolition of an old building and the leaving of its site empty for years in gap-tooth fashion. This bad habit was reproved as long ago as 1298 by Edward I when he had made York his capital, and the city corporation itself took strong measures against it between 1524 and 1587 on at least 14 occasions, on the specific ground that the resulting appearance of such open sites 'defaseth the Citie'. Dilapidated houses had to be repaired on pain of forfeiture and imprisonment was the lot of those who refused to repair houses which they had deliberately unroofed. We need not idealize the corporation of Tudor times, but their sense of what was due to the dignity of the city cannot be faulted.

The parish churches present yet another type of problem. In York, one of the cities with the largest number of small parishes, the surviving churches are far too numerous for the congregational needs of the central city. This has been recognised for many years, but little was done. Several churches had been demolished during the sixteenth century, and at least two others were ruined in the siege of 1644. The rest of the mediaeval fabrics survived until modern times, but in some cases suffered extensive 'restoration' or total rebuilding in the nineteenth century. One of the finest of the city churches, the fifteenth-century St Crux, had been pulled down in 1884–6; Christ Church in King's Court, largely Victorian, was cleared away in 1937. St Mary, Bishophill Senior, was demolished in 1963, after a long period spent in vain attempts to save it and to put it into sound repair. This final loss at last roused public opinion and led to serious reconsideration of the whole question so far as it affected York. On a national scale the redundancy of churches was

1. *Ferdinando, 2nd Lord Fairfax (1584–1648), conqueror and preserver of York. Owing to his strict control after the surrender on 16 July 1644 the city and the Minster were saved from damage. Antiquities were carefully rescued.*

2 Top *York as you go to Water Fulford, 1703, by Francis Place. A view from below the confluence of the Ouse and Foss.*
3 Above *The Noble Terras Walk of York, 1756, by Nathan Drake. Much the same view, but showing the new avenue along the east bank, begun in 1731 and extended in 1738–40 to form one of the most splendid of all such promenades.*

already under review, and York was chosen as the place for a pilot study. At the end of 1964 the Archbishop of York appointed a commission, under the chairmanship of Mr Marcus Worsley, to study the future of the city churches, and reports were published in 1967 and 1969. Under the new Pastoral Measure the work of finding uses for churches no longer needed parochially has been taken over by a diocesan committee appointed for the purpose.

Albeit slowly, uses for the churches or means of maintaining them are being found. A diocesan Youth Centre has been placed in part of St Martin-cum-Gregory, Micklegate, and this makes it possible for this fine building to be kept open for public inspection. Holy Trinity, Goodramgate, for which a special body of Friends had been formed in 1967, has now been splendidly repaired by the Redundant Churches Fund, and is also open. After detailed consideration of many schemes for St Sampson, at the heart of York's market area, it is being refitted to serve as an Old People's Centre, as recommended by the Worsley Commission. There seems to be a good prospect of maintaining St Saviour's and St Mary, Castlegate, for useful purposes. In all cases the serious difficulty arises over the delay in reaching definite solutions: the churches mostly remain closed and their condition steadily worsens, enormously inflating the cost of repair.

York was very properly made the subject of one of the four pilot surveys sponsored by government in 1967, to find solutions to the problem of historic towns throughout the country: 324 in Britain as a whole, according to a list prepared by the Council for British Archaeology, which regarded 51 (40 of them in England) as of national concern. Concurrently with the preparation of the York survey by Lord Esher there was legislation providing for Conservation Areas, and York was one of the first cities to publish a preliminary scheme, some 12 months before the belated publication of the Esher report. The report, which provided a cut-and-dried solution to the problems of the city within the walls — Lord Esher's terms of reference had deliberately excluded anything beyond the walls — led to prolonged controversy ending in only partially effective acceptance of what was meant to stand or fall as a whole. Matters were further complicated by the production of several successive schemes for an inner ring-road to take traffic around the city and relieve the 'historic core' of noise, pollution, and danger to residents and shoppers.

The provision of at least a bypass for York was nearly 50 years overdue. Any such roads would involve the provision of new bridges over the Ouse, and the various suggested sites became the battledore and shuttlecock of local politics for more than a generation. Again York's ironic genius played its accustomed part: a plan involving long approach roads in a 'middle ring' position and a bridge at Clifton was laid out and in part completed, but the bridge was not built. A fresh decision was made, that the approach roads were unsuitably placed, and new housing was accordingly built across their lines. Finally Clifton Bridge was built and opened in 1963, but as it has no effective approaches gives little help in solving traffic congestion. Ten years later the construction of the south-eastern section of an outer bypass was started, and is now in full swing. In the meantime, in 1971, a definitive scheme for part of an inner ring-road was put forward for the benefit of grant aid. Its revolutionary character produced the biggest uproar of any issue in York since the attempts of the Corporation to demolish the walls between 1799 and 1855.

The Walls were saved by the determined action of private citizens, led by the painter William Etty, who came from London by stage coach to take part in the protest. Nevertheless three of the four barbicans were destroyed, that outside Micklegate Bar in 1826, though Sir Walter Scott had offered to walk from Edinburgh to London to save it. No such dramatic actions have yet been recorded in the fight against the Ring Road, but the threat called into being a new society, York 2000, pledged to sane development of the city with an eye on the probable state of affairs by the year AD 2000, rather than on the short-term demands of the motorist. The growth of the new body was phenomenal: in less than four months it was able to present a formal objection to the Secretary of State with 3,729 signatures; and its membership had reached 9,200 when a Public Inquiry began on 17 October 1972, and 9,500 when the Inquiry ended on 6 December. Expert evidence was called in support of the objection by York 2000 and among the long list of other objectors the York and North Yorkshire Society of Architects, the York Group for the Promotion of Planning, and the (national) Ancient Monuments Society were prominent. At the time of writing, no decision has been handed down (20 months after the end of the Inquiry): nothing less than the fate of York as an historic city hangs in the balance.

The fundamental objection to ring-roads as applied to historic cities is that they positively encourage the growth of traffic. This is intensified in the case of proposals such as that for the York Inner Ring, where an urban motorway was planned for cars only, bicycles and pedestrians being excluded. Pedestrians would cross such a road by lengthy tunnelled underpasses, so that the effect of the ring would be divisive and anti-social, apart from the widespread destruction of a broad swathe of houses and shops for the road itself and for its junctions. Examples of such rings elsewhere, such as that at Chester, show vividly how they transform a genuine historic atmosphere into that of a preserved museum piece. Even the 'historic core', whose preservation was intended to be secured by the ring outside the walls, would lose by an unnatural divorce from its equally historic suburbs without the bars. Last but not least, the actual historic approaches to the city would be interrupted and the majestic entries through Micklegate and Bootham Bars would be lost for ever.

With such a background in very recent history it is inevitable that the present view of York should be a troubled one. There are, however, some grounds for cautious satisfaction. In the last quarter-century, since the war, an immense programme of consolidation has been carried out by the corporation upon the walls and bars; they have probably not been in such sound condition, overall, for 500 years. After a long struggle with the vested interests of London, York has won its fight for the National Railway Museum, and the building now approaches completion. Based on an existing engine shed, no longer in use, the museum has magnificent walls of blue engineering brick, and is likely to be one of the few positive additions to the York scene in the twentieth century. Another such addition, though not an architectural one, is the completion of the first section of riverside walkway from Ouse Bridge to Lendal Bridge. After many years this is, hopefully, only the beginning of a concentration of interest upon York's fine river frontage, neglected since the formation of the fashionable New Walk below the city in the eighteenth century. Some day there may be no hint of the ridiculous in comparisons with such water-borne cities as Paris, Venice, Stockholm, or Ulm.

The repair of the Minster and reconstruction of the Guildhall have already been mentioned, as well as the part played by the University in revivifying worthy old buildings within the central area, notably the palatial King's Manor, and the improvement and vigorous extension of the Theatre Royal. Ratepayers' money has been well spent on the two great museums, that in the Castle buildings and that, formed by the Yorkshire Philosophical Society, amid the ruins of St Mary's Abbey. Both of these are housed in fine buildings and are collections of outstanding importance, visited by great numbers of citizens and tourists throughout the year. Both museums contain material of the highest importance to scientific research in different fields, the Yorkshire Museum in particular having been the primary venture of the society (the YPS) which was the parent of the British Association. Not only the museum but the nobly wooded grounds in which it is set, and the well tended remains of York's second minster, are a treasured possession and an oasis of green calm close to the river.

The Museum Gardens, founded on the old 'Manor Shore', the precinct of St Mary's and later gardens of the King's Manor formed from the Abbot's Lodging by Henry VIII, were in origin a botanic garden. In their early days they benefited from the availability in York of one of the greatest firms of botanical nurserymen in the country, Thomas and James Backhouse of the Friars' Gardens, the site taken for the first railway station in 1839. The brothers Backhouse, Quakers from Darlington, had taken over the nursery as a going concern in 1816 from the Telfords, who had been running it for four generations since 1695. The Telfords, and their predecessors the Whartons, were concerned in such projects of the eighteenth century as the planting of the New Walk and the improvement of the Knavesmire, as well as the making of parks and afforestation throughout the North. A strong tradition of plants and trees therefore existed in York, and is responsible for a great deal that is best in the impression that it makes on the visitor.

The daffodils on the ramparts in spring have been mentioned, but they are only a part of the story. The grass verges of the main Tadcaster Road leading by the Knavesmire to The Mount are scattered with crocus, and nearer to the bars the cobbling between the main carriageways and the pavements is interrupted at intervals by fine trees. These plantings are the work of the Corporation, which also decorates the city with flowers in pots and baskets every summer, radiating from the glorious window-boxes of the Mansion House in St Helen's Square. Public institutions and private occupiers follow suit, not merely with baskets and boxes of flowers, but with a great deal of colour decoration in good taste. Here again the Corporation has set a good example with the treatment of the Mansion House and the civic offices in the Regency crescent of St Leonards opposite to the Theatre, and the redecoration by British Railways of the station for the Queen's visit of 1971 gave scope to aesthetic satisfaction as well as loyal appreciation of the renewed heraldry of the old North Eastern Railway. With these touches of colour, artificial and natural, we must live in hope.

2 The Perambulation of York

I Without

We are approaching York from the south-west by the old road from Tadcaster. Crossing the river Wharfe at Tadcaster, the point where the sovereign used to be met by the Lord Mayor and escorted for the last nine miles, we see on our left beyond the church a great viaduct. This now stands all dressed up with nowhere to go, for it is the startling relic of the direct railway from Leeds, that got half-way and then went bankrupt. The road climbs out of the valley and at the first milestone swings right off the Roman line for two miles, picks it up for a few hundred yards, then sweeps to the left for three miles. On the left is Bilbrough, with Fairfax's tomb in the chapel of an otherwise rebuilt church; and behind the manor house the mound, Marvell's mountain and model for the world. Two miles on, in a beautifully cultivated estate, is the Institute of Agriculture and Horticulture; a little further and lanes lead to Copmanthorpe on the right. The mediaeval and Roman roads once more unite, passing the nature reserve of Askham Bogs on the left, then the route is carried over the two railways, from the Midlands and from London by way of Selby. A lane descends swiftly towards Bishopthorpe, the archbishop's favourite seat since de Gray bought the manor early in the thirteenth century.

The last two miles are a straight run in, through the long street hamlet of Dringhouses, now heavily infilled with modern housing and preserving little of its former charm until the grand open space of the Knavesmire is reached on the right, and the smaller stray, or common, of Hob Moor to left, beyond the railway lines. In Dringhouses, now somewhat beset by motels, is the little church built in 1847–9, unusually elegant and well detailed for its period, by Vickers and Hugall of Pontefract.

York is before us, but cannot yet be seen because of the gentle eminence of The Mount, not so termed in ridicule but because it bore a defensive fort, known to engineers of the seventeenth century as a 'mount'. In the siege of 1644 it guarded the approaches so well for the King that this suburb alone escaped destruction. All the other roads leading in to the bars were lined with burnt-out houses that paid no rates for years afterwards. Before advancing into the area of older houses, inside the former boundary which divided the jurisdiction of the Lord Mayor and commonalty from the Manor of Dringhouses, we may stop to consider the historic nature of the great settlement that lies ahead. Like most ancient centres it has grown in successive skins, spreading outwards from the core within. Regeneration, redevelopment, and the rebuilding of single houses, also takes place within, so that the centre is heterogeneous. Externally, the most recent houses are mostly those that lie furthest out, and we plunge deeper into history as we approach the city gates. Of course urban spread was never precisely controlled, and fields and plots were sold haphazard by different owners. So our spatial advance is not uniformly retrograde in time, but by a sort of leapfrog or backstitch progress.

From the Knavesmire to the top of The Mount all the surviving houses belong to the nineteenth century and the older stratum mainly to the period 1820–40. This was ribbon development of a charming and semi-rural kind, and both larger and smaller houses are set back from the road with gardens in front. The houses on the left opposite to the Knavesmire entrance were built on land, Fishmonger Close, sold by the city in 1837, and the modern St Aubyn's Place has filled up the next field, Seggy or Marsh Close, which was also corporation land. Almost all the other development was on private freeholds or the trust property belonging to churches and almshouses. The large house on the lower corner of The Mount and Love Lane, now much extended as a hotel, is Elm Bank, built about 1870 but famous for its *art nouveau* interior inserted in 1898 under the York architects W. G. and A. J. Penty, and the Glasgow designer George Walton.

On the right at the foot of the hill is Newington Place, three houses built in 1823–7, but the larger detached villas higher up are the result of development of 1833 and the next few years and represent the most recent style of gentleman's residence in York at the time the railway was being projected and surveyed. One of these, No. 125, was occupied for a time by William Gray (1815–83), secretary of the York & North Midland Railway, before he moved in 1850 to a more modest home in the Holgate Road, now Nos. 70, 72. This had been built four years earlier and belonged to Mr Shafto, a builder, very likely the speculator who had erected the terrace. Back to The Mount: on the left, now in front of a modern house, is a brick wall with gate piers that belonged to the vanished Mount House, a solitary mansion of the eighteenth century. The fields around and behind it, The Mount Closes, were open land until late in last century and still are largely taken up with the grounds of the famous Mount School for girls of the Society of Friends. Beyond this Dalton Terrace now runs off on the left at the summit, having the Roman Catholic church of the English Martyrs, in watered Byzantinesque, on its right.

Here we have reached the top of the hill and look down the broad thoroughfare of The Mount and Blossom Street to Micklegate Bar, an archway of the twelfth century with upper works of the fourteenth, though shorn of its outer barbican as already told. On our left, upon the remains of the military mount, there stood for a long time the wooden post-mill seen in William Lodge's engraving of 1678. Lodge's views and others by his friend Francis Place show the wide rutted street sloping down towards the city, with no building nearer than the old St Catherine's Hospital which stood where Nos. 120–4 are now. To the right the nearest house was even further off, the predecessor of St Stephen's Orphanage, No. 89, formerly the home of John Dales, Lord Mayor in 1816 and 1829, and later of William James Clutton the well-known land agent and philanthropist. It was probably Dales who built the existing house and called it 'The Cottage'.

After the time of Lodge's and Place's views, but before the engraving of 1731 by John Haynes, another house was built on the south-east side nearer the brow of the hill. This is called 'Nunroyd' and in this century has been enlarged by the addition of a third bay-window; the two bays further from the city are original work of the rebuilding of the front about 1797. Occupiers of the old house included Thomas Hungate, a herald-painter, who inherited a baronetcy in 1749 but did not use the title 'being a man of penurious habits and of reserved and singular manners'; and two of the York clergy. After the refronting it was the home of the widowed Mrs Bedingfield from Micklegate, grandmother of Charles Waterton the traveller. It was Norman Green, the Lord Mayor of 1911, who enlarged the house. Alongside Nunroyd runs Mill Mount, the old lane which led to Mount Mill. Some distance down the lane on the right is Mill Mount School, which includes the unusual mansion built in 1850 for Charles Heneage Elsley, Recorder of York, by the architect brothers, John Bownas Atkinson and William Atkinson.

Facing Nunroyd is a short terrace of five houses, Nos. 136–44 The Mount, built in 1824 on Shepherd's Close, a field belonging to the feoffees of the parish estate of Holy Trinity, Micklegate. Beyond them is the narrow entrance to Mount Parade, one of the most charming and retired back-waters of York, a development of the same period, begun about 1823 and filled in by 1860. This was perhaps the first of a new idea in one-sided streets, facing the sun and with gardens on that side, at times across the approach street, a cul-de-sac with no through traffic. At the far end, on an irregular plot with a commanding view down the Holgate Road, stands Holgate Terrace of 1827. The good gardens and old trees still lend distinction to this little close of the latest Georgian. The final section of the Holgate Road, though now run down and in need of a facelift, is a pleasant back-door into York and still has character. This would be lost altogether and the district rendered uninhabitable if the monster junctions contemplated for the ring-road were ever built.

Returning to The Mount and proceeding downhill we pass a handsome series of houses, built individually side by side and not as a terrace, of 1833–49. The land surrounded the old Hospital but belonged to the merchants Leonard Simpson and John Simpson. At the petition of the Simpsons a new almshouse was built to designs by George Townsend Andrews on a site at the back facing the Holgate Road, since they were 'desirous of selling or leasing the frontage towards (The Mount) . . . for the purpose of building several new houses'. The Corporation, responsible for the old hospital, agreed. The final section of The Mount, down to the junction of the Holgate Road, was the part which had been largely built up from an early date, and really formed the outer end of Blossom Street. Of several old farmhouses to

be seen in engravings and watercolours the only survivor
now is Nos. 82–6, on a much bigger plot acquired by the
town clerk Robert Davies in 1835. Davies built his own
large house, Nos. 88, 90, on the uphill frontage of garden in
1851 and installed his widowed sister, Mrs Skaife, in the
older house, which preserves a patterned Dutch gable at the
end of a wing projecting at the back.

Above the Davies property are seven late Georgian and
Regency houses set close together. Highest up the hill is a
group of three built in 1807, dated by the discovery of a
Roman tomb when the foundations were dug. These have
shallow bow windows going up two storeys and their brickwork has been painted to imitate a stucco finish. They took
the place of an old farmhouse whose cowsheds stretched
along the next plot, where two smaller brick houses stand,
perhaps incorporating part of the old wall of the sheds.
Below these is a pair of houses built in 1821 by Joseph
Bullock, a brickmaker, and then sold. They have wide
shallow bow windows of imposing scale flanking paired front
doors, and were designed in other respects to look like a
single large house. Most of these were the homes of professional men and artisans: in No. 102 there lived for a time
Elizabeth Frank, the friend and biographer of the Quaker
grammarian Lindley Murray, and in No. 98 two sisters of
Henry Cave the York artist. On the opposite side of the
street is the Abbey Park Hotel, recently much extended but
preserving the fine brick house of 1832 designed for Alderman William Dunslay by Peter Atkinson (1776–1843) the
father of the brothers J. B. and W. Atkinson. Its main front
faces Park Street, where the first house on the left was built
in 1836 by Thomas Rayson, bricklayer and building con-
tractor, for his own occupation. This again was laid out as a
parade, with a large garden opposite to the front of the house,
beyond the carriageway.

Next to Park Street is a tall terrace of four houses of 1831,

and below them late Victorian shops on the site of the ancient
Sun Inn. The Bay Horse public house still survives, though
a few years ago it would have been pulled down or altered
beyond recognition had it not become a favourite meeting
place of members of the University. Possibly built in the
first instance as a farmhouse in the period of reconstruction
after the Siege, it was an inn before the middle of the eighteenth century. Its sign is first mentioned in 1798 and may
refer to the racehorse Bay Malton which in 1765 won the
famous Gimcrack 500 guineas at York. George Benson, the
architect and local historian, was the son of a former landlord
and spent his childhood here.

After the junction of the Holgate Road on the left, once
Holgate Lane, there used to stand the timbered range of
Barstow's Hospital, an almshouse, but in the later nineteenth century this gave place to shops, and on the land
behind was built The Crescent in 1868–9. In the second
house lived the Revd James Raine, chancellor of the Minster
and historian, and his son Angelo Raine was born there on
Michaelmas Day 1877. Then come the Odeon Cinema of
1936 and the Prudential Assurance Building already mentioned. These modern changes have taken away much of the
architectural interest of this side of the street, but opposite
a good deal survives to show the historical York pattern of
large and small, dignity and impudence side by side.
Stretching away to the right are the 20 fine houses of the
long terrace called South Parade, a venture of the York
Commercial Building Company and built in 1824–8. Peter
Atkinson the architect lived in No. 17 as its first occupier,
and in No. 16 next door was Thomas Rayson the builder, so
that it is pretty certain that they were responsible: the design
and technique in any case resemble their known works.

A grand run of houses stretches on towards the Bar,
beginning with the Lion and Lamb of 1828 and ending with
some excellent late Georgian houses and the Bar Convent

with a fine brick front of 1786–9 by Thomas Atkinson, a contemporary but no relation of his fellow architect Peter Atkinson the elder, father of the Peter already mentioned and partner of John Carr of York. The complex architectural history of the Convent and of the adjacent houses which belong to it has been worked out in detail by Dr E. A. Gee. The almost palatial buildings, intended from the first to be a school for girls, form a striking part of the social history of the city since the Reformation. In spite of periods of anti-Catholic disturbances the recusant community was generally respected and at most times interference was kept to the legal minimum. The first Superior was Frances Bedingfield of the Norfolk family, which also sent to York Edward Bedingfield (1730–1802) who, as we shall later find, lived within the Bar at No. 114 Micklegate. The house next door, No. 19, was occupied by William Hotham, Lord Mayor in 1802 and 1819, until his death in 1836, when it became the chaplain's residence. In No. 21, largely rebuilt in 1845, lived George Leeman, MP, but of greater interest is the short occupancy of the older house on the site, between 1824 and 1831, by James Backhouse the Quaker botanist and nurseryman. From its front door he left for the epic ten years' mission to Australasia and South Africa, from which he returned with the material for a classic, his *Narrative*, and many rare plants and seeds.

The Prudential, on the left of the street, abuts on the much older house now the York Railwaymen's Club. It was built as a pair by the wine merchant John Horner in 1789, and had a large warehouse behind it. The houses had some distinguished residents, including the first Joseph Rowntree (1801–59) and the architects Charles Watson and James Pigott Pritchett between 1807 and 1831. Finally, at the corner of Queen Street is the picturesque Windmill Inn, built in the seventeenth century and known by its present name since 1735, when the heirs of Henry Lee sold it to the occupier. Lee had been a miller at one of the Mount mills, as had four generations of his family before him, from 1621 and it is evidently to this link that the inn owes its sign. Like the Bay Horse up the street, this building had a very narrow escape from destruction in the recent mania for redevelopment.

The entry to the Bar was widened in the latter part of last century, but there formerly stood on the corner of Nunnery Lane the mediaeval Hospital of St Thomas, amalgamated with the Corpus Christi Guild in 1478. As an almshouse it survived the Reformation and was transferred to the city, but the building at last fell to the pickaxe in 1862. From the higher ground at the foot of the Bar we can look back through Blossom Street and up the long vista of The Mount, still a noble view in spite of the losses of the recent past. Here was space for the old horse and cattle market, held on the cobbled strips at the sides, and here too may have been a hiring fair for servants, suggested by the derivation of the name 'Blossom' from *Ploxswain*, a ploughman. Numerous as are the inns and public houses still, there used to be many more, and the ordinary man of business, as distinct from visiting gentry, commonly found his hostelry here.

Later on we shall circle the walls and pass within the city, but first must explore the other roads leading towards the Bars. Only one of these is of outstanding interest, the route from Scotland entering through Bootham. On this side York had no ancient jurisdiction comparable to the Ainsty: there is no Tadcaster ten miles out, no street village like Dringhouses. Until late in last century the North Riding came into the built-up area to take in the precinct of St Mary's Abbey right up to the Walls. Those same northern walls of the city were the boundary of the Forest of Galtres in the Middle Ages. The road for a long way into York runs almost dead level through the Vale, and not far from the course of the Ouse. Coming from Northallerton, Thirsk,

and Easingwold the outer ring of the suburbs is touched at
Skelton, where the exquisite thirteenth-century church lies
a furlong to the left. Two miles on and the closely built
modern suburbs begin, and quite suddenly we reach Clifton
Green on the right. Here is a small oasis, sadly disturbed by
through traffic to the new bridge, but with a number of
pleasing small houses of the eighteenth and early nineteenth
centuries, and the modern but picturesque public house,
The Old Grey Mare.

Further on and beyond the former cinema is the one
architecturally interesting building, the old Manor House
known as Nell Gwynne's House, with 'Dutch' gables and a
front of rusticated brickwork with projecting windows like
oriels. Soon after this is the corner of Burton Stone Lane,
with the historic – or prehistoric – Burton Stone marking the
limit of the old jurisdiction of the city on this side of the road.
On the right or west side was the Liberty of St Mary's within
the North Riding. The land remained open until a relatively
recent date, and has the very early Victorian Gothic St
Peter's School and later houses of little interest. On the left,
which lay within the city, there is older development which
becomes notable after the bridge over the railway to Scarborough. Opposite, just before the bridge, stands Ingram's
Hospital, an almshouse built by Sir Arthur Ingram shortly
before the Civil War and with a rebuilt Norman doorway
which may have come from Holy Trinity Priory in Micklegate. Opposite, set back from the street, is a large square
house (No. 65, called Record House) built for Miss Barbara
Ashton Nelson in 1827 and regarded with some justification
as one of the sights of York when it was new.

After crossing the railway Bootham Park is on the left,
a magnificent open space with grass and trees, intended to be
bisected by the ring road in front of John Carr's noble
Hospital, the County Lunatic Asylum of 1772–7, a little
later than Carr's great project for the hospital of Santo

4 King's Staith, with Cumberland House on the right, seen from Ouse Bridge by the lens of William Henry Fox Talbot in 1845: one of the first photographs of the city.

5 Lop Lane and the west front of the Minster, with the Red House on the left; another early photograph.

6 Top left *Micklegate Bar from without*; 7 right *Monk Bar from without*.
8 Above *Walmgate Bar with its surviving barbican.*

Antonio in Oporto, a foreign commission which he presumably obtained because of his contacts with the local family of Croft of Stillington, in the port wine trade. Another design by Carr is a little way down the street, No. 47, built about 1753 for Mrs Mary Thompson, widow of Edward Thompson who had been MP for York for twenty years. The whole group of eighteenth-century houses, now taken over by Bootham School, is very fine. On the other side of the street No. 54, a handsome house of grey brick with a Doric portico, was the home of Dr George Auden, physician and scientist, and in 1907 the birthplace of his son, Wystan Hugh Auden the poet.

The city, or north-east side of Bootham was one of the most select districts of York in the great age of routs and assemblies, notwithstanding the noise of the traffic on a main road. Some houses were built for members of county families, other were speculations intended for fashionable letting during the season; but most of the work was of very high quality. The main block of Bootham School, No. 51, was designed by Carr's junior partner, Peter Atkinson the elder, for Sir Richard Vanden Bempde Johnstone, Bart, and built in 1803. Nearer the Bar, No. 33 was apparently a speculation of the master builder Robert Clough in 1754, but it is mainly of importance as the home of the astronomers Nathaniel Pigott and his son Edward Pigott, who discovered Pigott's Comet while living here in 1783. On the other side of the street is the opening of Marygate, formerly an independent hamlet in St Mary's Liberty and still an attractive way to the church of St Olave, the Museum Gardens and the bank of the river. To the left of the narrow lane is the Marygate Tower, the angle turret of the precinct wall of the abbey. The wall had been started in 1266 and heightened after 1318; the angle tower was added some few years later. It became a muniment room after the dissolution of the abbey, and contained the vast collection of records taken from Yorkshire monasteries by the Court of Augmentations. During the Siege of York the Parliamentarians mined the tower and blew it up on 16 June 1644, with disastrous results for the documents, though many were saved from the ruins. The tower was repaired afterwards, but because of the Bootham houses built against it, the new work does not bond with the old and the clumsy break is now obvious after demolition of the houses this century.

The project of clearing the outer face of the abbey wall was undertaken in 1896 and a few houses have been removed at intervals when leases fell in or some other suitable opportunity arose. Few of the buildings have any architectural interest, and the scheme may be applauded as leading eventually to a brighter street with a band of gardens and turf at the foot of the wall, which would greatly relieve the present somewhat claustrophobic gloom of Bootham as it narrows on approaching the Bar. The impression of gloom is heightened by contrast, since there is an ample space on the left, after passing Marygate, in front of the Old Maids' Hospital. This is an almshouse founded under the will of Mrs Mary Wandesford for ten poor gentlewomen who never married, of the Church of England, 'who shall retire from the hurry and noise of the world into a Religious House or Protestant Retirement', and was built in 1739–43. The extent of retirement from the hurry and noise of the traffic amounts only to 50 feet, but even this is well worth having. The wider sections of Bootham are only 60 feet between the houses as against 80 feet on The Mount and nearly 100 in Blossom Street: the greatly increased amount of disturbing noise in houses next to the narrower street can be vouched for by those who have worked in both.

Close to the Bar the traffic is particularly bad, for the stream from the North crosses that coming down Gillygate on the left. For many years Gillygate, the street named after the long vanished church of St Giles, has been the victim of planning. The justified attempt to clear St Mary's walls of decrepit and uninteresting houses fired an imaginative project for opening up longer stretches of the City Walls and grass ramparts. This was incorporated in a town plan for York prepared in outline in 1948. The plan, which included proposals for an inner ring-road and much that was purely visionary, has ever since underlain civic thinking. One detail of the plan involved the total destruction of all the old houses of Gillygate and the formation of a new road clear of a turfed rampart and moat below the Walls. Unfortunately no consideration had been given to the individual houses of the old street: not all of them should be destroyed. For 25 years the area has lain under a blight and even the better properties have been allowed to decay; but at last, perhaps too late, the Esher Report and the outcry over the 1971 ring-road proposals have produced second thoughts. Before passing on, we should glance at a few buildings in Gillygate which ought to be preserved.

At the corner of Bootham are two pairs of houses of great historical and architectural interest: Nos. 15, 17 on our left, and Nos. 3 and 5 in Gillygate. These were built by Thomas Wolstenholme, a carver and maker of architectural ornaments moulded in composition, who told the story in his will made in 1800. 'I . . . from the beneficence of my Creator have been blessed with Health and Genius which aided by Industry and Economy enabled me in the year 1790 to purchase of Mr John Hudson a freehold estate situated at the corner of Bootham and Gillygate in the parish of St Giles . . . upon part of which premises in the year 1797 I built two houses fronting into Gillygate and also in the year 1799 erected a small house facing into Bootham . . .' Wolstenholme, a member of a remarkable family of York craftsmen, left No. 5 Gillygate to his daughter, and states that he had fitted up No. 3 as his own residence, but it was to pass to his youngest brother Francis, who was to succeed to the business 'in Composition Ornaments, Carving, and Gilding, with all the Stock in hand, moulds, drawing tools, books (etc.) . . . in the shops' at the King's Manor or elsewhere. The immense premises of the Manor were at the time let out by the Crown on leases to all sorts and conditions.

Not far up Gillygate on the right, numbered 18 and 20, is the home of the great York artist Joseph Halfpenny (1748–1811), who lived here for many years and died in the house. Halfpenny shares the credit with his more famous contemporary John Carter (1748–1817) of having been the first to understand the real character of Gothic detail so as to depict it accurately. He was the son of Thomas Halfpenny, the archbishop's gardener at Bishopthorpe, who was one of the founder members of the Ancient Society of York Florists in 1768 and probably responsible in 1774 for the planting of Knavesmire Wood with its vista from Bishopthorpe Palace to the old church at Dringhouses. A little further up Gillygate on the same side are Nos. 26 and 28 which, like No. 33 Bootham, were built by Robert Clough. Both houses have had distinguished occupiers, including the Revd John Kenrick the classical scholar and a founder of the Yorkshire Philosophical Society, who lived here from 1823 to 1848.

Bootham Bar lost its barbican in 1831 but, after a sharp tussle, was saved from demolition and restored three years later, though extensive repairs have been done on several subsequent occasions, most recently in 1970. To the right opens St Leonard's Place, cut through the Walls and old housing in 1831 and now a major traffic artery. Later developments included the formation of Exhibition Square with the City Art Gallery but, mercifully, the postern gate of the abbey precinct was spared. Though generally called 'Queen Margaret's Arch', this is a misnomer. Henry VIII's sister, Margaret Tudor, stayed in York in 1503 on her way to Holyrood to marry James IV in the dynastic union which led to the Stuart succession in England. Margaret, only 13 at the time of her marriage, made the famous remark on this occasion: 'How sweetly the bells of York do ring'; but she stayed in the Archbishop's Palace, not the Abbey. The truth, discovered by Robert Davies long ago, is that the postern was not made as a convenient exit for Margaret in 1503, but in 1497 when the Abbot of St Mary's was expecting her father, King Henry VII, to stay with him while visiting York.

From Bootham Bar to Monk Bar the best walk is along the top of the Walls, as we shall see; but outside the ramparts it is possible to go up Gillygate and then turn right through Lord Mayor's Walk, formerly a quiet and pleasing street, shaded by trees (elms were first planted in 1718) and with the city ramparts and grass-clad moat on one side. Now doing duty as a section of inner ring-road, its peace is lost. What is almost incredible is that, in the 1971 plan for 'half an inner ring-road', Lord Mayor's Walk was to serve as a main traffic artery for the future. On behalf of the planners of 1948 it must be said that they had never suggested this. The further end passed through an area of mediaeval suburban development, Newbiggin (the 'new building'), to reach Monkgate outside Monk Bar. Just outside the Bar stood St Maurice's church, replaced by a Victorian building in 1876. This became redundant in less than a century and the site was cleared in 1966, providing space for a large traffic roundabout.

There are several curious features of layout in the alignment of Monk Bar, Monkgate, and the old church of St Maurice, built late in the twelfth century. It has been pointed out by Mr H. G. Ramm that there must have been a Roman road from the *porta decumana* of the fortress, in the middle of its north-eastern wall, to the site of Monk Bridge over the Foss; and that in the earlier Middle Ages a road is likely to have run on much the same alignment. Old St Maurice's church, not orientated precisely, was parallel to a road in that position and should, therefore, have been laid out before the present Monkgate or the present opening in the Walls at Monk Bar. The removal of the city gateway from the Minster precinct, the layout of Monkgate from the new opening to Monk Bridge, and the curious street-plan internally would be connected with the building of stone walls on the ramparts after the middle of the thirteenth century. The suburb of Newbiggin, set out at right angles to the walls, as shown by the parallel lines of Groves Lane and Love Lane on each side of – but not parallel to – Monkgate, was therefore of intermediate date, probably in the twelfth century. Monk Bar itself is of the fourteenth century and does not show any sign of there having been an earlier stone gatehouse.

The entry to the city from Monk Bridge is not of outstanding beauty though Monkgate is a pleasing wide street until, like Bootham, it narrows to the Bar. Coming inwards most of the better houses are on the left or east side of the street. George Hudson the Railway King lived in No. 44, which he largely rebuilt during his period of glory as MP and Lord Mayor of York in 1837 and 1846. Hudson inherited the property in 1827 from his uncle Matthew Bottrill who, in 1796, had taken out fire insurance on the old house described as 'brick built and tiled' for £300. Earlier owners had been, in the seventeenth century a coverlet weaver, then a cordwainer; in the eighteenth an apothecary who sold it to a yeoman, whose son-in-law Joseph Beckett was a butterweigher. Beckett's widow in 1760 disposed of the house to a most interesting personality, Thomas Beckwith the painter (1731–86), who was an archaeologist in advance of his time and who made large collections with a view to a revised edition of Drake's *Eboracum*. His friend Edward Abbot stayed with him in 1774–6 when writing a history of York Minster which survives in manuscript, and while making a large number of watercolour sketches of buildings, often the only record of what has been lost in the last two hundred years. Beckwith's son, a doctor of medicine, sold to Bottrill, described as a gentleman; his nephew George Hudson was, of course, a linen-draper.

Beyond Hudson's house are several fine brick houses built in the eighteenth century, and then the courtyard of the County Hospital. The open space is now regrettably cluttered with minor and temporary structures, but behind them stands the grand block of the main building, built in 1849–51 to designs by J. B. and W. Atkinson, the last architects to maintain the Georgian tradition in York, as might be expected of the heirs in practice of John Carr. Before reaching the Bar, St Maurice's Road – the old Barker Hill – runs downhill on the left, outside the ramparts. Some way down is St Maurice House, now a Nurses' Home, a fine example of the York house with paired bow windows and perhaps the first of its kind. It was being built in 1792 for James Lamb gent., who had a lease for 40 years from the Vicars Choral of the Minster. As we have seen, the rather similar 'Nunroyd' near the top of The Mount was not built until some five years later than this.

St Maurice's Road continues downhill as Jewbury, which actually was next to the site of the burial ground of the Jews of mediaeval York, though 'bury' is really the unrelated word *burh*, used to describe an outer suburb. The Walls on top of the rampart to the right of the road are a fine sight here, but the beautiful Layerthorpe Postern and Bridge, seen in old paintings, have long disappeared, victims of the corporation's campaign against the Walls in 1829. The subsidiary road into the city at this point, Layerthorpe, needs no itinerary, and it is better to continue around the city by Foss Islands Road. This in fact fills a gap in the line of Walls where, in former times, there was the open water of the King's Pool or Fishpond. As this is part of the circuit of the defences, to be described later, we are here concerned only

with the far end of the road, at the surviving barbican of
Walmgate Bar.

The eastern way into York is the Hull Road, now running
through districts of modern development until it reaches, at
the point where the thoroughfare becomes St Lawrence
Street, the site of the mediaeval Hospital of St Nicholas. The
buildings were ruined in 1644 during the siege and nothing
now remains, except for what was saved by Fairfax. He had
the splendid Norman doorway, dated by Professor George
Zarnecki to *c.* 1160, taken to the parish church of St
Margaret, Walmgate, and rebuilt there as a south porch.
Three of the bells were likewise sent to the church of St
John, Micklegate, where they still hang, though in a steel
frame. The old frame was dated 1646, confirming the
transfer at Fairfax's orders. Two of the bells have good
Lombardic inscriptions commemorating Lady Beatrix de
Roos who died in 1414 and Thomas de Walleworth, Master
of St Nicholas Hospital, who died in 1409. A quarter mile
nearer the city is the large churchyard of St Lawrence
containing the unduly large Victorian parish church of
1883–92 with a tower and spire most unsuitable in terms of
regional style. Closer to the street is the modest tower of the
old church, preserved at the demolition. Another fine
Norman doorway, from the nave, is rebuilt against the tower,
which dates from the thirteenth century. The upper stage, a
good example of Tudor Gothic, has been dated by bequests
in wills to *c.* 1502–9. These remains are all that is left of the
church in which, on 14 January 1718–19, Henrietta Mariah
Yarburgh of Heslington Hall married (Sir) 'John Vanburgh
of Castle Howard', the great palace which he designed for
the third Earl of Carlisle.

Little of architectural merit survives on the last of
the main roads entering York, that from Selby through the
village of Fulford. Fulford is indeed charming, but from the
old boundary of the city most of the way is built up with

modern houses and institutions. On the right are the Barracks of the Northern Command, with some original work of 1795–6, set back from the road and with a later Infantry Barracks to the south. The road bears left, but off Cemetery Road to the right is the Cemetery of 1836 with a fine chapel designed by J. P. Pritchett, already mentioned. To the left of Fishergate is New Walk Terrace, running towards the river, with a few houses of interest. On the right of the street, in front of No. 73, is the rebuilt Piazza originally built in front of the Theatre Royal in St Leonard's Place. When the Theatre was refronted in 1879–80 the arcade was taken down and re-erected here. Another turning on the left is Blue Bridge Lane, leading down to the river and the tree-lined New Walk along its banks. On the left of the lane is Fishergate House, a curious mansion of 1837, comparable to Elsley's Mill Mount House. The street forks again, and while Fishergate bears to the left past the former Rialto Cinema and the immense glass works, it is Fawcett Street on the right that actually leads to Fishergate Bar. The remains of some good old Georgian houses are mostly altered for the worse, and the general impression is not distinguished. The site of the glass factory was that of the precinct of St Andrew's Priory and for long remained open ground known as Stone Wall Close.

At the end of the street, before it turns left over the navigable Foss, is the Fishergate Postern Tower, one of the most picturesque relics of the defences, beyond a stretch of walls set high on their rampart at the southern angle of the city. The buildings of the Castle rise on the left and are in impressive contrast to the garages, petrol pumps, and factories of Piccadilly, the most thoroughly unhistoric street in York.

3 The Perambulation of York

II Walls and Monuments

Again we stand at the foot of Micklegate Bar. This time we are to make the round of the Walls, at least of the city's defences, for York neither has nor ever had a complete circuit of stone walls. Not only were they cut by the river at two points, but for 500 yards their place was taken on the east side by the King's Pool, as we have seen. The Foss, far wider than the navigable channel is now, again interrupted the line between Fishergate Postern and the Castle. Of the stone walls that once existed, the greater part survives, but the section from Baile Hill to Skeldergate Postern has been cleared away, as has that south-west of Bootham Bar, where St Leonard's Place was carried through. The section from Lendal Tower and past the Multangular Tower to the break at St Leonard's Place is not accessible for walking, nor is it possible to walk on the walls of the separate precinct of St Mary's Abbey, outside the western angle of the city. None the less, the walls and the roads and bridges which join the various sections, provide a magnificent promenade, mostly free from the problems of crossing traffic, and also a fine view of most parts of the city and of many of its chief buildings.

The whole of the defences and their history are described by Dr R. M. Butler in his full and scholarly account, and little need here be said. For our purpose the walls provide a convenient path from which buildings and prospects may be spied as we move round York in a clockwise direction from start to finish. The fact that it is possible to use these military works for the pleasure of a promenade is a measure of the pacification of England. All the same, it is surprising to find that the use of the walks for amusement goes back to the early years of the eighteenth century, in part to the general restoration of 1719 and subsequent years. By 1736 the corporation decreed that in future leases of the ramparts 'a liberty of walking on the Walls . . . shall be excepted'. In the same year Drake refers to the completed repairs of the whole of the wall south-west of the river, from North Street to Skeldergate Posterns, and on the other side of the Ouse from Fishergate Postern to Walmgate Bar, stating that 'these were of late years levelled upon the plat-form, paved with brick, and made commodious for walking on for near a mile together; having an agreeable prospect of both town and country from them'. Parts of the remaining walls were still leased out for private gardens, preventing what was to be wished, that 'a walk of this kind, like that on the walls of *Chester*, might be carried quite round the city'.

Whereas the Roman fortress was completely surrounded by stone walls, and the *colonia* or civil town almost certainly was also, these did not constitute the circuit of the much larger mediaeval city. Moreover, before the Norman Conquest most of the Roman walls had been broken down and the stumps had been covered by earthen ramparts. These did surround the greater part of the urban area, continuing the Roman north-east and south-west walls, of the fortress and *colonia*, in a south-easterly direction and turning to reach points on the banks of the Foss at Layerthorpe and the Ouse at the bottom of Skeldergate. The south-eastern defence was probably for a time the Foss, from Layerthorpe to the Castle, built by 1069. By that time Walmgate existed as a street, and there may have been a defensive bank to this bridgehead on the line of the later parish boundary of St Denys; but by soon after 1150 there was almost certainly a rampart on the line of the later Walmgate walls of 1345 and thereafter.

The stone walls as we know them were begun about 1250, just after Henry III had started the rebuilding of the Castle in 1245. The archbishop's castle of the Old Baile on the south-west bank was provided with palisades until soon after 1327, and the stone wall around the Walmgate quarter was built from 1345 onwards. Before the building of the walls, stone gateways had existed in the ramparts otherwise of earth and with timber palisading. The archway of Bootham Bar may even be as early as the end of the eleventh century and the whole lower stage of Micklegate Bar belongs to early in the twelfth. An upper storey was to be built in 1196. Part of the surviving masonry of Walmgate Bar is of the middle of the twelfth century and the stone bar certainly existed not later than 1161. The present Monk Bar is not earlier than the fourteenth century but, as has been mentioned, there was probably an earlier gateway on the line of Chapter House Street and near the *porta decumana* of the Roman fortress.

In the year 1137 there was a great fire in York on 4 June which burned the Minster, St Mary's Abbey, the great Hospital on the site of the Theatre Royal, and 39 other churches; and another fire soon afterwards destroyed the church of Holy Trinity in the suburb of the city – Holy Trinity Priory in Micklegate. To make up the number of 39 churches it is necessary to include even those early parish churches which stood outside the line of the defences, and this clearly shows that sparks could be driven over the banks quite easily in a way that would not have been likely once the tall stone walls existed. The whole aspect and contour of York in that earlier period must have been completely different from the picture we know, and which has endured more or less for the last 600 years or at any rate since 1389, when there was already a wall between Walmgate Bar and the King's Pool. This was the last stretch on which a wall came to cap the earthen bank: the provision of the whole of the Walls had taken more than a century.

Looking at the outward face of Micklegate Bar as it is now, we see two lesser arches on the left and one on the right. The single archway of the bar itself was the only way through from soon after 1100 until 1753, when a single arch for pedestrians was made on the west side; this was replaced by the present pair of arches in 1863; on the east side the foot passage was made in 1827, when the gateway was restored after losing its barbican. On passing through the western-most arch to the left, steep stone stairs climb first to the level of the passage above the main archway, then to the walltop. From the landing level there is an excellent view down the great street of Micklegate, curving away majestically towards the right. At the top we are among the upper branches of the trees which grow on the inner rampart but can look down on the busy traffic in Queen Street through the battlements. The grassy slope of the outer rampart, facing the sun, is covered by the finest crowd of daffodils in spring and, all the year round, there is a magnificent weeping willow hiding the backs of the houses which look sideways at the Bar.

On the short walk to the south-western angle of the city we may catch a western breeze and glimpses of a distant horizon over the railway sheds towards Holgate. Below and to our right is the street which keeps the name of Toft Green, though the old green has long gone. It was the only large open space, a couple of acres, inside the walls on the south-west of the Ouse. The Black Friars, whose precinct was that of the old royal palace just to the north, wished to take in part of the green in 1307 but were refused permission because on that plot and nowhere else the assembly of the people to show arms could be made; there was a common market held there for strangers and indwellers from time immemorial; it was the place of duel in case of trials by combat for felony; and furthermore it was the only place in the whole city for erecting military engines in time of war. It was also called Pageant Green from the sheds used for storing the 'pageants' or scenery used for the stages of the Mystery Plays. This was during the Middle Ages the only cattle market in York, and there was a horse-market every Thursday. Until the early years of the nineteenth century there was still a swine market, held on Wednesdays, but the ground was then taken over to build a prison, the House of Correction, in 1814.

Prison, market, pageants, the Black Friars, and the great nursery which succeeded to their gardens, are all gone and the railway since 1839 has reigned in their stead. The buildings of the Old Station still stand, used as offices, but the rails and the train shed in 1967 gave place to the new headquarters of British Rail's Eastern Region. The massively repetitive block of concrete and glass, the result of a more positive attitude to design than has recently been common, is none the less horrifying in its likeness to an inspection hive – the date '1984' seems to loom as we see the myriad workers at desks within. As a contribution to the delayed rehabilitation of the Railway King, this has been named Hudson House. As we turn the corner of the walls and face northwards we cross over the two great mock-Gothic arches which let the rails through: the first is the later, made in 1845; the second on our route was cut in 1839. Parallel to us on our left is the front of the new Railway Station opened in 1877, and beyond its northern end the great mass of the Royal Station Hotel, dominating large gardens sloping towards the bank of the river. The road beneath hums with traffic and crowds throng the shelters waiting for the infrequent buses for the suburbs.

Just beyond the zebra crossing which allows passengers to walk from the station across the traffic into the city, is a long narrow oasis of trees and grass, scattered with a few tombstones. This is the Cholera Burial Ground formed for the victims of the ghastly epidemic of 1832. As a public open space that now softens tragedy into a tranquil resignation, the Burial Ground is of enormous value at this point. Typically, a ruthless attempt to seize the ground for road-widening was made in 1923–7, but was defeated after two years of resolute battle by the single-handed efforts of the Yorkshire Architectural and York Archaeological Society (the 'Yayas'), York's oldest amenity association, founded in 1842. Inside the wall, below on the right, stands the North Eastern Railway's memorial to their staff who fell in the war of 1914–18; through the archway and a short distance off, by the river outside, is the larger City War Memorial; both were designed by Sir Edwin Lutyens. The railway memorial stands close to the fine Refreshment Room block of the Old Station, built in 1840, and the old Station Hotel of 1852–3, both designed by G. T. Andrews. Surtees, who had at first opposed railways, became reconciled by the swift transport to the hunting field and in later life came to regard the York Station Hotel as the best in England.

Facing the old hotel is the North Eastern Railway headquarters building of 1900–6 by Horace Field, in its day regarded seriously but now amusingly Edwardian in a frivolous way and far more acceptable than the cleverness of Norman Shaw or the pomp of Sir Aston Webb. It has been regrettably outweighed by the looming block of the Yorkshire Insurance on the corner of Rougier Street. On the other side of the street is a smaller but still unwieldy block of offices. The wall-walk, though switchbacking over the arches which have been cut at various dates to allow the roads in and out, is tending steeply down towards the Ouse, and a noble view of the Minster lies ahead. It is common to have to stop to avoid interference with the many photographers from this favoured point. In front are the trees of the Museum Gardens, framing the tall Lendal Tower on the opposite bank. The tower became a waterworks in 1616, was fitted with a Newcomen steam engine in 1755 and improved by the great engineer John Smeaton in 1784.

On the near side of the water, to our left as we join the pavement of Station Road just before Lendal Bridge, is the North Street Postern Tower beside the steps which led to the old ferry. Between the two opposing towers was hung a chain to defend the waterway from 1380 or earlier until 1553. Crossing the bridge there are good views both up and down the river: to the left the Water Tower of the St Mary's precinct can be seen as the far limit of the gardens, and beyond it the Scarborough railway bridge of 1845 and 1874. Downstream on the far bank are the delightful boatyard and house beneath the Victorian Yorkshire Club of 1868, then the river front of the municipal offices and the Guildhall of 1447–53 by the master mason Robert Couper. Above modern buildings peeps the surviving tower of St Martin in Coney Street. Looking back at the south-west bank, the Viking Hotel of 1965–7 now dwarfs the charming group of the spired church of All Saints, North Street, rising behind mediaeval timbered houses. In the foreground anglers are commonly seen fishing from the bank.

Beyond Lendal Tower a stretch of the wall runs up the hill to the Lodge of the Museum Gardens, but its walk is not now accessible. Beyond the Lodge is a gap filled by the gates and railings of the gardens as far as the ruined St Leonard's Hospital of the thirteenth century. On the right is the street of Lendal, really a continuation of Coney Street and representing the riverside main street of the Roman *canabae* and later of the Viking city. Museum Street continues to the cross-roads of St Leonards Place and Blake Street, with Duncombe Place beyond exposing a good view of the west

9 Top left *Looking up Stonegate towards the Minster;* 10 right *The Shambles early this century, showing the butchers' shops.*

11 Above *The narrowing view from Bootham towards the towers of the Minster above Bootham Bar.*

IMP·CAESAR
DIVI·NERVAE·FIL·NERVA
TRAIANVS·AVG·GER·M·DAC
CVS·PONTIFEX·MAXIMVS·TRIB
NICIAE·POTESTATIS·XII·IMP·V·COS·VI
PORTAM·PER·LEG·VIIII·HISP·FECI

12   Above *The Trajanic inscription recording the building of the south-eastern gateway of the Roman fortress in AD 108.*

13   Right *Successive walls: the mediaeval city wall on the left was built on a new alignment outside the Roman fortress wall, ruined and by then buried beneath a rampart of earth. The Anglian Tower, centre, stands in a breach of the Roman defences; beyond it the successive ground levels have been marked in section.*

front of the Minster. Following the line of the walls as
closely as possible we enter the gardens and beyond the
ruined Hospital see a stretch of the Roman fortress wall on
the right and beyond it the Multangular Tower. Its small-
scale original masonry is capped by an upper stage with
battlements added late in the thirteenth century. Leaving
the Yorkshire Museum and the abbey ruins ahead on our
left, we turn right around the Multangular Tower to enter
the narrow lane between the rampart of the city walls and the
precinct wall of the abbey on the left. Immediately on our
left is the severe post-Georgian front of the Curator's House
of 1844 by J. B. and W. Atkinson. On the right a footpath
leads through a small postern doorway in the city wall to the
Anglian Tower and the associated stretch of the broken-
down Roman wall, here on an alignment a few feet within
that of the mediaeval stone wall which was taken down to a
separate foundation. Beyond the Anglian Tower the levels
of various periods have been well marked out and show
vividly the different epochs of the defences.

Most of the abbey precinct wall is now incorporated in the
late mediaeval buildings of the Abbot's Lodging, the core of
the later King's Manor. Opposite to the point where, on our
right, the city wall breaks off at the cut of 1831, the Lodgings
show the brickwork and terracotta – a very early instance of
its use in the North – of the work begun in 1483 by the
master bricklayer Richard Cheryholme with his four
servants. Cheryholme had taken up the freedom of York as
a tiler in 1481, but probably originated in the clay-working
area near Drax where his surname is found as far back as the
fourteenth century. We emerge from the lane into the open
space of Exhibition Square, with St Leonard's Place in an
elegant crescent on our right and the Theatre Royal with its
recent extension opposite, to the right of the De Grey Rooms
of 1841–2 and the Conservative Club. At this point a family
of peacocks from the Museum Gardens may sometimes be

seen crossing the road in the midst of traffic, to reach the
pleasant little garden by the Theatre.

Leaving the King's Manor behind us and on the left the
Principal's House of 1900 in Carolean style by Walter
Brierley, a successor in practice to Carr and the Atkinsons,
we pass the statue of William Etty amid recent fountains in
front of the City Art Gallery. Ahead is the Abbey Postern or
'Queen Margaret's Arch' and bearing right, across the road,
the outer front of Bootham Bar. Here we can once more
climb to the wall-walk up a steep staircase added outside the
wall, entering the upper room of the Bar. The portcullis,
though now fixed, still exists in raised position. Emerging
on to the top of the wall running to the north-east we have
trees growing thickly on the rampart on our left, in the back
gardens of Gillygate. On the right, over the gardens and
roofs of the Close, are glimpses of the west towers and north
side of the Minster. Further on can be seen the remains of
the old Archbishop's Palace and its Chapel, built about
1233, now the Minster Library, amid fine lawns and trees.
Towards the northern angle is the modern brick Deanery in
a good garden extending up to the walls.

From the Robin Hood Tower at the north angle we get a
view over the rather desolate western end of Lord Mayor's
Walk and the northernmost houses of Gillygate. Turning to
the right along the north-eastern walls splendid views of the
north side of the Minster open up among the trees. Through
the battlements on our left are the fine avenues of Lord
Mayor's Walk, beyond the grassed moat, and on the other
side of the Walk the buildings of St John's College, the
diocesan training college of 1841–6. Beyond the Deanery a
large group of earlier buildings stand between us and the
Minster: the residences of Minster Court and then the huge
rambling palace which until Henry VIII's confiscation
belonged to the Treasurer of the Minster. It is now divided
into two parts: Gray's Court, which includes much of the

mediaeval building and is used by St John's College; and the Treasurer's House, owned by the National Trust. The gardens between the Walls and these houses are particularly fine. We descend towards Monk Bar and go down a steep narrow staircase to the street.

Another staircase rises opposite to the walls leading towards Layerthorpe. From the walk outside the Bar we look outwards over the turfed site of St Maurice's church towards modern blocks of buildings at the beginning of Monkgate. Further on, and beneath us to the right, are the exposed foundations of the eastern Roman angle tower of the fortress; but the mediaeval wall continues straight ahead. The timbered gable of the Merchant Taylors' Hall appears below to the right, and on the left we look across through the battlements at St Maurice House of 1792 with its tall bow windows. A large area at present lies open between the inner face of the walls and the street of Aldwark, and is being investigated archaeologically before new building takes place as part of Lord Esher's plan for the rejuvenation of the derelict area. Certain fine old buildings have been, or are being, restored. Looking back from this stretch of wall are some of the noblest prospects of the Minster, with its east front rising above the houses. At the New Tower, so called in 1380, we turn sharply left, following a salient of the wall behind the churchyard of St Cuthbert's, Peaseholme Green. Across the grass ramparts to our left is Jewbury; beneath the wall on the right is the charming garden now maintained by the Borthwick Institute. There are good views looking back at the outside of the Walls from the salient, before we descend to the street level at the point where, in 1829, Layerthorpe Postern was hacked away.

Crossing the street, with views to the right past St Cuthbert's church to the Borthwick Institute in the fifteenth-century St Anthony's Hall and, on the left, the picturesque Black Swan inn, we have to turn left, then right, into Foss

Islands Road. This provides a promenade along the left bank of the River Foss Navigation, across the site of the King's Pool. On our left is York Power Station and, across the water, a good modern cooling tower, with a pleasing landscape of dwarf weeping willows along the bank as foreground. The Foss sweeps away to the right but we go on past several blocks of excellent modern housing in brick before reaching the Red Tower. Here the line of the mediaeval walls begins again, on what was the southern edge of the Pool, with a brick tower built in 1490 by the York tilers. This caused a demarcation dispute with the masons, and a tiler, John Patrik or Partrik, was murdered and the cathedral master William Hyndeley and his assistant Christopher Horner charged with the crime; they were later acquitted.

From the Red Tower to Walmgate Bar the walls are very low. Within are occasional views, through blocks of new housing, of the tower of St Denys's and of the east front of St Margaret's church. At the Bar we have to go down to the street, cross Walmgate, and climb again on the other side. The inner face of the Bar is cloaked by a curious timber-framed projection built during repairs in 1584–6. In the house above the Bar was born John Browne (1793–1877), the historian of York Minster and draughtsman of distinction. This is the only one of the four Bars to keep its barbican, of the fourteenth century, as well as its portcullis and wooden doors, dating from the fifteenth. Outside the next section of the walls there were until recently the pens of the Cattle Market, but these have been cleared away and the rampart turfed, with admirable results. As we leave the Bar there is a good view to the left along the wide sweep of St Lawrence Street and the top stage of the old tower of St Lawrence's church; to the right of it is the tall broach spire, ridiculously out of place, of its Victorian successor. Below us is the front of the Spotted Cow inn, on the site of the mysterious Ace House, traced back by Angelo Raine as far as 1575. It seems possible that it was connected with the preparation of potash for use by the York dyers.

We descend once more to cross George Street at the simple arched Fishergate Bar, perhaps built in its present form, more or less, about 1400 but blocked from 1489 to 1827, when it was restored. Beyond the Bar the wall kicks out-wards, then turns sharply to the right, to end at the Fisher-gate Postern Tower of 1504–7. Here we leave the walls to cross the streets and the widened Castle Mills Bridge. On our right rises the Castle; below us on our left are the bottom locks of the Foss Navigation. The roadway bears to the left to cross Skeldergate Bridge, with good views of the Castle and Clifford's Tower on its mound behind and to the right. To the left of Clifford's Tower can be seen the short section of the Walls between the destroyed Castlegate Postern and the river bank. Here, as at the Lendal ferry, there was formerly a chain hung across the river to the Skeldergate Postern Tower, first mentioned in 1403 as the tower next to the Crane, which stood on the common wharf beside it, and was demolished in 1878. On the east bank of the Ouse, from the Walls southwards, runs the splendid New Walk planted with elms and limes in 1731. Later replantings have ensured that the view, as seen from Skeldergate Bridge, remains magnificent. Across the bridge we look right into the bottom of Skeldergate, until recently a picturesque street but now denuded of all but a couple of Georgian houses. Nearly 100 yards of the wall was destroyed in 1878 and we climb to the walk at the foot of Baile Hill, the site of the second Norman castle raised by William the Conqueror in 1069 but later maintained by the archbishop as it stood within his fee.

The mound of the Baile stands inside the wall on our right; on our left we look down from a considerable height on Bishopgate Street and what was once the village of Clementhorpe, now covered with warehouses and factories.

The wall turns to the right at the Bitchdaughter Tower, the southernmost angle of the defences, and slowly climbs back towards Micklegate Bar. The district on our right within the Walls is Bishophill, an area associated with the mediaeval 'archbishop's fee' or 'shire' but earlier known as Bitchill, possibly accounting for the name of the angle tower. We cross over the archway of Victoria Bar, made in 1838 on the site of a small arched postern called Lounelith, the 'hidden gate', as early as the twelfth century. The street which passes through the Bar, now Victor Street but formerly Lounelithgate, led to the west front of St Mary Bishophill Senior, now gone. The trees of its churchyard can still be seen from the wall. As we proceed the large Norman tower — on a Saxon base — of St Mary Bishophill Junior becomes prominent on the right. This was the early church of St Mary Bishop, part of the ancient endowments of the Church of York, along with its parish inside and outside the walls, a large area which included much of suburban York and the villages or hamlets of Copmanthorpe, Holgate, and Upper Poppleton. As we near the Bar, the extensive buildings of the Bar Convent can be seen across Nunnery Lane on the left. At the foot of the inner rampart on our right, along the street of small houses called Dewsbury Terrace, ran the wall of the precinct of Holy Trinity Priory. Just before reaching the Bar the tower of Holy Trinity appears between the late-nineteenth-century housing built over the precinct after 1854. We are back at the Bar, and descend the steep steps to the great street of Micklegate.

4 The Perambulation of York

III Within

York can only be savoured on foot and those who wish to appreciate and understand the city must be prepared for lengthy wanderings. The beauty and the historical interest are well spread out, though concentrated particularly along certain routes. Much of the way suffers from the intensity of modern traffic and, for walks within the walls, it is as well to avoid the rush-hours of morning, mid-day, and evening. The sights are often on both sides of the street, and it is necessary to cross and re-cross. We can only hope that in time much more of the streets will be devoted to walkers, as Stonegate is already. For the time being, and for those with limited time, the preferable side of each street will here be suggested: preferable for walking, in that the most visually exciting buildings and scenes are opposite.

Setting out once more from Micklegate Bar and with the Bar behind us we begin on the right-hand side. There is little to see here in the upper part of the street, but a grand sweep of houses of different sizes and dates starts soon after Bar Lane has led to Toft Green, and bears gently to the right. The Roman line has been abandoned and we follow the route towards the bridge that grew up after the Dark Age floods. The way this side of the river leads across three parishes, now united but still keeping a little of their older flavours. Here on the highest level – the summit is 65 feet above datum – is Holy Trinity, the parish of the mediaeval priory but in former times also known as St Nicholas. As if the monastic aura had taken long to fade, this was for three centuries after the Dissolution much frequented by the distinguished families of the old faith. Their outward venture was the Bar Convent beyond the gateway; here they lived quietly to themselves, excluded from politics and public office.

The series of historic houses on the north-west side of the street begins with the long range numbered 142–6, which belonged to the Waller family and was built largely by Robert Waller, Lord Mayor in 1684 and MP in 1690. Later it came into the family of Gage, probably responsible for the top storey about 1810. No. 138 belonged to the Fothergills; No. 136 was the town house of the Goodricke's of Ribston Hall, who owned the Trinity Gardens across the road – the old precinct of the Priory – but the present front was made after 1883 when it was Franks' Hotel. The next house was the home of Henry Jubb, Lord Mayor of 1773, a locally famous doctor, and afterwards of the York banker Robert Swann. The brick house Nos. 118, 120 was built *c.* 1742 by Robert Bower, a mercer, but he sold it to one of the St Quintin family of Scampston. Another Lord Mayor, George Peacock, proprietor of the famous *York Courant* newspaper, lived here from 1806 to his death in 1836: his two mayoralties of 1810 and 1820 saw the start and finish of the present Ouse Bridge. The street begins to be interspersed with some smaller and less significant houses, but No. 114 was notable for its occupants. Edward Bedingfield (1730–1802) of the ancient Norfolk family, settled in York on his marriage to Mary Swinburne of the Northumbrian family to which the poet belonged. The Bedingfields' daughter Anne married Thomas Waterton of Walton Hall and became the mother of the great naturalist and eccentric Charles Waterton, author of *Wanderings in South America*. After the widowed Mrs Bedingfield had moved to 109 The Mount (see above, p. 42), the house was let to Richard Hansom, a carpenter, the grandfather of Joseph Aloysius Hansom, born here on 26 October 1803. Hansom, architect of the Catholic church of St George in York, of St Philip Neri, Arundel, and of the Birmingham Town Hall, was also founder and first editor of *The Builder* weekly in 1842 and inventor of the horse-drawn cab which bears his name.

The small house next door was an ancient endowment of the Vicars Choral of the Minster and for a long time the Red Lion public house; behind the undistinguished front it is a timbered building of the sixteenth century. The Nag's Head too, at No. 100, hides an old house of the fourteenth and sixteenth centuries behind its brick front. The carved sign on No. 94 is the only relic of the great Falcon Inn, ruined by the railway and reduced to half its old frontage as a public house in a rebuilding of 1842. Beyond it are three houses, among the gems of the whole street. No. 92 is of the last two or three years of the eighteenth century and is typical of the work of John Carr and his junior partner, the elder Peter Atkinson, rather stiff and even prim, but obviously of the highest quality. The older house had belonged to yet another Lord Mayor (of 1715), Captain Robert Fairfax, RN, who was MP for York in 1713; the present building was for his grandson. Later on it was the York home of Thomas Backhouse, the elder of the two nurserymen brothers, from 1817 until he died in 1845, when he was succeeded by his brother James (see above, p. 46) until 1859.

The great pile of Micklegate House dominates the scene. Built for John Bourchier about 1750–2 as his town house, it is probably an early work of John Carr, when he was still quite as much the master mason as the architect. It overtops its neighbour on the east, Bathurst House, and formerly did so in a far more noticeable way. Bathurst House, when built about 1720 for Charles Bathurst the High Sheriff of Yorkshire, had only two storeys, and got its present attic only about 1820. The original building, in a lovely dark brick that positively glows, is one of the greatest gems of the Georgian period. The first house in the parish of St Martin-cum-Gregory, its plot runs alongside Barker (or Gregory) Lane, through which carriages withdrew to the coach-houses and stables at the rear, facing upon Toft Green and Tanner Row. On the other side of the lane was the little church of St Gregory in mediaeval times. Because of its frontage on the whole length of the lane, Bathurst House can be identified as standing on a piece of land given early in the thirteenth century to maintain a canon in the priory of Healaugh Park 'for ever'.

Meanwhile, on the right-hand side of Micklegate, we have been passing by a series of ancient houses that stand on the frontage of the precinct of Holy Trinity Priory. Before reaching Priory Street, Nos. 99–103, the Coach and Horses, are all that remain of a range of houses built in the fourteenth century to the west of the old Priory gatehouse pulled down in 1854. Beyond the gap is a later range, three-storied, of timbered houses with jetties at first and second floors. It may be that they owe their survival to use by butchers, just as in the case of the celebrated Shambles on the other side of the river: the continuous tradition of the trade has required little alteration to premises. In any case they are a notable example of the way in which, towards the end of the Middle Ages, crowded cities of two storeys were being rebuilt with a third storey, the beginning of the upward march to the skyscraper blocks of today. In London the change was in progress from soon after 1300, but elsewhere such development was uncommon for another 200 years.

The churchyard of Holy Trinity, rising high above pavement level, opens out to the right between the street and the north side of the church. With its fine trees and its spring flowers the open space is a welcome oasis. By the church path is a set of stocks with five holes, the subject of many York jokes and silly stories, notably the one about the persistent offender of an unspecified period who had only one leg. The fine tower, which includes re-used details of the twelfth century, was built by the parishioners of St Nicholas against the Priory nave in 1453. There was a much larger central tower, but after the dissolution it was blown down in the great gale of 1552, and destroyed what was left of the choir. Through many vicissitudes the surviving fragments of the nave and old crossing have come down to our day, and enough of the design is preserved to show that the nave was a crisp example of very early Gothic in typical northern style.

In Trinity Lane, a narrow alley opposite to Barker Lane on the other side of Micklegate, the first house on the right is the former public house called Jacob's Well, now a parish room. Built towards the end of the Middle Ages by the Priory, it came into the hands of Isabel Warde who had been the last prioress of Clementhorpe Nunnery. Before her death in 1569 she gave the house to the feoffees of the parish church: that part of the nave of the priory church in which parochial rights had survived the monastic establishment. Much more interesting than any part of the original house is the carved timber porch, consisting of a pair of brackets made in the fifteenth century and brought here from Davygate across the Ouse. Brackets of this kind were, up to a hundred-and-fifty years ago, a special feature of the ancient buildings of York, but these are now unique. Further down the lane on the same side are the much altered remains of 'Towers' Folly', a soap-boiling factory built about 1638 by Nicholas Towers, Sheriff of York who died in 1657. Much later it became a horn and comb factory and then a private house. It was the birthplace of the Victorian authoress 'John Strange Winter', really Henrietta, daughter of the Revd Henry Vaughan Palmer. A little further on, the street of Bishophill Junior on the right leads to that church.

Retracing our steps to Micklegate and turning to the right, we are looking down the steep hill by which the street drops to the bank of the river through some 30 feet. This central part of the street belongs to St Martin's parish and was occupied largely by merchants and small traders, though there were a few houses of distinction too. On the left, at the corner of Barker Lane, is a row of small houses built in 1821 as a parish investment, to designs by the younger Peter Atkinson. Beyond these are smaller houses with Georgian fronts but sometimes concealing remains of much earlier structures. In No. 68 lived the noted glass-painters Edmund Gyles and his son Henry Gyles, who continued until his death in 1709 the last of the tradition of mediaeval glass in the city. Henry was also a distinguished member of the artistic and antiquarian coterie which centred round Ralph Thoresby of Leeds. The common ground between men of different social strata in eighteenth-century York is noteworthy.

The next house of major quality is No. 54, the town house of the Garforths of Wiganthorpe, built in 1755–7 and probably by John Carr, in the same style as Micklegate House. Almost precisely opposite, on the right-hand side of the street, is another house in the same style Nos. 53, 55, built about 1754 for Lady Dawes and her second husband, Paul Beilby-Thompson, but noted as the residence of the Countess of Conyngham, a great benefactress of York, who died at the age of 91 in 1816. We have, however, overshot several houses with interesting associations nearer to Trinity Lane. The house, now two shops Nos. 69, 71, was built in the sixteenth century but has a front of *c.* 1750. Until 1830 part of the premises formed the Minster Inn, mentioned by Drake in 1736 as 'of good resort'. Another part was the home of the Revd Philemon Marsh, rector of St Martin-cum-Gregory for 43 years until his death in 1788; his family crest appears on a rainwater head. Next door downhill No. 67 was over a very long period a butcher's shop. The two houses above Lady Conyngham's mansion are both of interest: first is No. 61, built late in the eighteenth century and probably for the nurseryman George Telford, occupier from 1786 to 1809. After the death of Colonel Charles Telford, the last of the family, in 1894, this was bought by Dr W. A. Evelyn, one of York's most distinguished antiquaries as well as a prominent medical man. Below, Nos. 57, 59 are really a single house built in 1783 and the home of Robert Swann the banker before his move to No. 128 on the other side of the street in 1801 (see above, p. 72).

Typically Victorian business premises stand beyond No. 53 and carry the block to St Martin's Lane on the edge of the churchyard of St Martin-cum-Gregory, one of York's most beautiful and unspoilt churches, in another oasis between the houses, shops and offices. The church fabric is of fine quality, built largely in the fourteenth and fifteenth centuries, but it also contains many fittings of interest. In 1548 the church was to be demolished and was stripped of its lead, but was saved by the determined efforts of the parishioners led by Alderman John Beane, who lived close by. There is some splendid glass of about 1335 and also, in the north aisle, curious windows painted by William Peckitt and his school in the second half of the eighteenth century. Scratchings on plain glass inserted by local glaziers in 1746, just after the '45, include such loyal sentiments as: 'I hope this may be a plase for true protestants to resort to & never to be ruled by Papists God Bless King George ye 2d & Billy off Cumberland Whome God long preserve.' There is a pulpit of 1636, an oak reredos made by Bernard Dickinson in 1749–51 and communion rails by Matthew Butler, of 1753.

In the street, next below the churchyard, is a pair of houses of 1835 by J. B. & W. Atkinson, who had their own office in No. 39 until 1851. Next below is a large house, Nos. 35, 37, on a site occupied by a stone mansion belonging to Hugh de Selby, Mayor in 1230. It passed through the families of Clerevaus and Scrope and early in the sixteenth century came to John Beane, already mentioned, Lord Mayor in 1545 and 1565. From him it descended to the Whartons who rebuilt the brick front in the eighteenth century. It was sold to Peter Atkinson the younger before 1812. He lived in No. 37 himself and then leased it to William Hargrove, proprietor and editor of the *York Herald* and an outstanding historian of York. Later still the surgeon Sir William Stephenson Clark, the Lord Mayor of 1839, was the occupier. The tall house now the Cromwell Hotel stands where another mediaeval mansion stood, the home of John de Hotham who later became Bishop of Ely and between 1320 and 1328 more than once Chancellor of England.

Beyond St Martin's we should cross over the street to the north side, entirely rebuilt in recent years except for the church of St John, closed in 1934 but restored. Only a few houses on the south side of the street now remain of the fine group of ancient mercantile buildings that until a few years ago faced each other across Micklegate. Part of another three-storey timbered building of the late fifteenth century, possibly a rent built for Fountains Abbey, survives behind the front of No. 21. In No. 13, a house built about 1740, lived the artist Henry Cave. Next to the east is the most splendid house in the whole street, or rather a pair of houses designed as one, Nos. 3–9, built for the family of Thompson, wine merchants, about 1720. Richard Thompson was Lord Mayor in 1708 and 1721, but the magnificent mansion became a grocer's private residence, then a grocer's shop; the other half was the Queen's Hotel from 1845 until a few years ago, but recent neglect has thrown a shadow on the future of one of the best buildings in the whole city.

We have reached the point where Micklegate ends and Bridge Street begins, at a cross-roads. To the right is Skeldergate, to the left North Street, forming a sort of 'Strand' a short distance away from the right bank of the Ouse and in Skeldergate including wharves and warehouses. Skeldergate is said to mean the street of the shield-makers, but there is no ground for thinking that they ever worked here, and it is more likely that it was the street that ran along a 'skeld' or shelf by the river. It used to contain many picturesque houses and a few of distinction, including that built by John Carr for himself but bombed in the war of 1939–45. Carr may also have designed No. 56, built for the merchant Ralph Dodsworth who had bought the property in 1769, but perhaps a few years later. Dodsworth was Lord Mayor in 1792. A little way further on is a good brick saw-mill of 1839 built for John Henry Cattley, who lived in No. 53 next door to it, an older house but much altered for him.

In the other direction, some way up North Street, beyond the new Viking Hotel, is the important parish church of All Saints, containing the best stained glass in York except for that in the Minster. The series of windows inserted in the first half of the fifteenth century is particularly fine, and its history has been unravelled in detail by Dr Gee. Two of the windows are famous for their subjects: the Fifteen Last Days of the world, and the Corporal Acts of Mercy. The first of these was almost certainly by John Thornton of Coventry, the artist of the Great East Window of the Minster. These are in the north aisle; on the opposite side is a window of the Nine Orders of Angels, reconstructed from a chaos of fragments after the fortunate discovery of a drawing made in 1670 by Henry Johnston and now at Oxford. There is much else to see internally, and externally there is a fine tower with tall tapering spire, doubtless suggested by the

larger spire of the Black Friars' church only a short distance
away. Around All Saints clusters a group of timbered
buildings of considerable beauty, and the area still conveys
an impression of mediaeval city life hard to parallel.

The eastern side of North Street has mostly been cleared
to the river and affords fine views of the Guildhall and the
commercial premises on the other bank, above them peeping
the tower of St Martin, Coney Street. As has been mentioned,
a riverside walk now runs beside the water back to Ouse
Bridge, beyond which it is possible to continue for the
length of the Queen's Staith, then turning up into Skeldergate, and by Albion Street or Carr's Lane to Lady Middle-
ton's Hospital, an almshouse rebuilt on this site in 1827–9
to the design of Peter Atkinson. Carr's Lane climbs the
steep declivity of the old river bank, between the Friends'
Burial Ground and the old churchyard of the demolished
St Mary Bishophill Senior. Turning right into the street of
Bishophill Senior we pass on the right the site of the lost
palace of the Duke of Buckingham prominent in seventeenth-
century views, then a group of old houses. The famous Dr
Stephen Beckwith lived in No. 19; next door No. 17 was a
cottage built just before 1755 by William Carr, a carpenter,
for himself; No. 15 was built for John Tuke, the surveyor, a
member of the well known Quaker family of York. Finally
comes Bishophill House, formerly one of the most distinguished in the city and with exquisite plasterwork in the
style of Francesco Cortese, probably inserted about 1765
when James Fermor took the house. His widow married
another William Carr, nephew of the architect John Carr.

From this point it is possible to return to Ouse Bridge by
Fetter Lane, to Micklegate by St Martin's Lane or Trinity
Lane; or to Micklegate Bar by way of Bishophill Junior and
Priory Street. Taking the first route we emerge upon the
bridge of 1810–20, designed by Peter Atkinson the younger,
to take the place of the ancient bridge seen in so many

14   Overleaf *Within the Minster nave, seen from the north-west. Designed by Master Simon, the nave was built in 1291–1322, and vaulted in timber by Philip of Lincoln between 1345 and 1360.*

15   Top *England's finest mediaeval dome: the wooden vault of the chapter-house dating from about 1285–90.*

16   Above *St Mary's Abbey in ruins: the north wall of the nave of 1288–94, contemporary with the completion of the Minster chapter-house.*

paintings and prints. The old bridge had been built in stone after a wooden bridge had collapsed in 1154 under a crowd gathered to welcome their archbishop – later canonised as St William of York – on his return from exile. The fact that no lives were lost in the disaster was regarded as his first and greatest miracle. A month later he was dead and rumour had it that William's enemies had slipped poison into the chalice used by him at Mass. Whatever the truth of his death, it gave York a saint and the Minster a shrine.

For more than two centuries the bridge was famous for its magnificent central arch spanning 81 feet, where two of the old arches and the pier between had been swept away by floods in the winter of 1564–5. Martin Bowes, a York man who had been Lord Mayor of London, sent Thomas Harper an expert mason from London Bridge to give advice. With the York master, Christopher Walmesley, Harper in two years succeeded in re-establishing communications over the new arch. Though far later than the Chinese Great Stone Bridge of AD 605–16, and only two-thirds of its span, the York arch was a remarkable achievement for its time, being seven feet wider than the Ponte di Rialto in Venice which, besides, was not built until more than 20 years afterwards. Like the Rialto Bridge and Old London Bridge, that at York was lined with houses and shops. These were gradually cleared away after 1745, but some remained at the eastern end until the last years of the eighteenth century.

In 1782 Dr William White, a physician and local anti-quary, made a sketch survey of the streets of central York to a large scale, starting from Ouse Bridge. He marked the relative sizes of houses and all the entries and lanes between them, with the names of the occupiers and their trade or profession. On the eastern bridgefoot there were still four shops on the north side: a cork-cutter, a paper-box manu-facturer, another cork-cutter, a watchmaker; and on the south a trunk-maker, a fruit and oyster shop, a stationer, and

Mr Fryars' inn called the Blue Anchor. The busy mixture of activity in Georgian York can be savoured by following White as he climbed Low Ousegate from the Bridge. On the left or north side were Clark watchmaker, the Fortune of War public house, Bussey basket maker, Bewlay shoemaker, Waud miller, an empty house, a meal shop, Ward bricklayer, Barwick butcher, Hartley flax-dresser, Burkell barber; and, after Church Lane, a house 'joined to the Bank 1789' and The Bank, Garforths & Co. taking up the corner site in front of St Michael's Church, as might be expected.

Coming up on the right side of the street White passed Mr John Dodsworth ironmonger and raff merchant, Gains hatter, Pinder clogmaker, Wilkinson druggist, Robert Bewlay shoemaker, Volans milliner, Easterby tobacconist, an empty shop, Astington's Turk's Head coffee-house, Mr Thistlethwaite, Mrs Beverley hardware shop, and Harrison's coffee-house on the corner of Nessgate. We cannot follow out in detail the whole of the route recorded by Dr White. He went on to the east along the ancient way: High Ousegate, Pavement, Hosier Lane; Spurriergate to the north and Nessgate to the south; then Castlegate, Castlegate Postern, Castle Mills, Fishergate and the road to Fulford, besides Coppergate, the twin street to High Ousegate between Nessgate and Pavement. White's interest in this central area was in part personal: on the north-east side of Castlegate between St Mary's church and the Castle he noted his own birthplace, 'Domus meus natalis' in what was Mrs Dodsworth's house in 1782, while opposite were the Quaker Meeting Yard, Beckwith's Yard and Mrs Beckwith, then 'My Aunt Grace Hamond's' and her garden behind the house.

There is little now to note in Low Ousegate, apart from some realistic model cats crawling on the walls of the buildings on the right, and St Michael's Church with the old clock on the left at the cross-roads. Time was taken from the bell of St Michael's as early as the 1390s, when the cooks of the city were not to buy 'fra evynsang ryng at Seint Michel kyrk at Osebryghend on to the morne that prime stryke at the Mynster'. It is the interior of St Michael's that, when accessible, is really worth seeing. Tall slender piers carry an arcade of the earliest Gothic: a trick, since the heightening of the piers was a rebuilding of the fifteenth century, when the old arches and details were preserved, perhaps from mere economy. The result is extremely fine. From the fifteenth century too is the stained glass, with another window of the Nine Orders of Angels, different in design from that reconstructed at All Saints.

At the crossroads we must stand and take stock of the parts of the inner city that still lie before us. Here we cross the main street of Viking and mediaeval York, which under five names: Lendal, Coney Street, Spurriergate, Nessgate, and Castlegate, is really one. Coney stands for Coning: this is the King's Street, the king's highway between the Castle to the south-east and the old palace of the earls of Northumbria where St Mary's Abbey was founded after 1085. Its line is essentially that of the civilian street of the *canabae* between the Roman fortress and the bank of the river. A great part of the street's length is within the parish of St Martin, always one of the richest areas in the city, as the church was unofficially the civic church. In joke the street is still called the golden half-mile. Though now mainly a shop-crawl, it is worth walking from one end to the other and noting the few outstanding buildings.

Starting from Museum Street, opposite to the Lodge of the Museum Gardens, the Judge's Lodgings are on the left, originally the somewhat eccentric private house built for Dr Clifton Wintringham about 1720. Opposite stands the building which was the Lendal Congregational Chapel, designed by Pritchett and Watson and built in 1815–16. It has been cleverly converted into a coffee-house below and restaurant above. Across a narrow lane is a group of good Georgian houses among which Nos. 10, 12 are excellent work of *c.* 1715–25 though with alterations. After the Post Office comes St Helen's Square, with the little church and the lower end of Stonegate on the left. To the right a gate leads down, beneath the Mansion House of 1726–32, to the Guildhall, one of the great mediaeval buildings of England. A short distance down Coney Street are the remains of St Martin's, with a large hanging clock of 1778 surmounted by the figure called the Little Admiral, a naval officer taking an observation through his telescope. Inside the restored south aisle a good deal of valuable stained glass – some from elsewhere – should be seen.

Most of Coney Street, though a busy shopping centre, is a gloomy chasm but it still has relics of its former grandeur. A single column on the right represents the new front of 1716 added to York's most famous hostelry, the George Inn, now otherwise utterly destroyed, though fragments of its timbered entrance are preserved by the Castle Museum. The street changes name to Spurriergate where Market Street, the old Jubbergate, runs uphill on the left. This leads to Peter Lane Little, named from the old parish church thus distinguished from the Minster, destroyed in the sixteenth century and now reduced to a short length of walling just above ground level and on private property. The southern end of Spurriergate brings us back to St Michael's church, surrounded by the picturesque Church Lane with a tiny yard and an old water lane leading down to the brink of the Ouse.

Pursuing this crosswise route through the very short street of Nessgate – the way to the 'ness' or headland between the two rivers Ouse and Foss – we leave the modern Clifford Street on our right and enter Castlegate. Some way along on the left is the church of St Mary with a magnificent tower and spire, apparently as much based on that of the Franciscans as that of All Saints North Street was inspired by the Dominicans' steeple. Beyond the closed church are two

notable mansions designed by John Carr, on either side:
Castlegate House of 1759–63 on the right, set well back;
and on the left Fairfax House, roughly contemporary but
perhaps begun a few years earlier. This was built for the last
Lord Fairfax of Gilling, belonging to a branch of the family
remote from those of Steeton famous in the Civil War and to
whom the Fairfax house in Micklegate belonged. Castlegate
House was the residence of Peter Johnson, recorder of York
for 30 years, 1759–89. Castlegate now ends in a melancholy
wilderness, a vast car-park beneath the grassy mound of
Clifford's Tower. Begun in 1245 for Henry III by Master
Henry de Reyns, this elegant quatrefoil was the keep of the
new stone castle built during the next 20 years.

Splendid views are the reward for climbing to the top of
the Tower and it is of great architectural importance as a
royal work of the mid-thirteenth century. Very little else of
the castle proper survives, but the three great blocks of
official buildings are noble works in their own right. In the
centre is the old Debtors' Prison, built as a county gaol in
1701–5; to the left the Female Prison of 1780 and later; and
opposite the Assize Courts built in 1773–7 to Carr's designs.
The Castle Museum is housed in the two prison blocks, and
in the old exercise yards of the Female Prison are the re-
erected fronts and shops of 'Kirkgate' and the other sections
of the Kirk collection of bygones, opened here in 1938 and
since extended. Between Clifford's Tower and the Ouse is
the former precinct of the Franciscans, with part of its river
wall as the only visible survival. Across it runs Peckitt Street,
commemorating William Peckitt, the reviver of glass-
painting, who lived here in a house overlooking the Ouse.
Going north along the King's Staith towards the Bridge we
see on the right the splendid Cumberland House of *c.* 1710–
15, at the foot of what was Middle Water Lane. In the
other direction we may take the delightful walk, beneath
Skeldergate Bridge and out of the city, for the whole length

of the New Walk along the bank, and on to Fulford Old
Church.

Back at St Michael's church we proceed uphill through
High Ousegate, a street largely destroyed in the fire of 1694.
Some of the houses may date from the rebuilding but most
are later: No. 5 is of 1743 and No. 11 of 1758. The rainwater head dated 1763 on No. 13 was probably added when
the corporation ordered that spouts were to be put up on all
houses pursuant to Act of Parliament. These houses, and
the best of the undated, are on the north side of the street,
but on the south is the church of All Saints, Pavement,
preceded by the open space formerly used as a Herb Market.
High above is the tower with its elegant open lantern, in
which it is said that a light was placed to guide travellers to
the city after nightfall. This church has been designated the
future parish church of the inner city on this side of the river,
and to it have been transferred stained glass and other relics
from closed churches now united to the benefice.

The street here changes its name to Pavement, the earliest
paved way in the city, and is crossed by the modern Parliament Street of 1833–6 and Piccadilly, made into a thoroughfare in 1910. Parliament Street was built as a wide market,
to supersede the old Thursday and Saturday Market places;
but it has in its turn given way to a new market-place formed
between it and The Shambles. Most of the houses on Pavement are now replaced by great stores, banks, and offices.
The jettied and gabled house called Sir Thomas Herbert's
is the chief survivor, but is not mediaeval. Though very
commonly said to be the birthplace of Sir Thomas, in 1606,
it was not built until rather later and by one of the Jaques
family who succeeded to the Herberts. Herbert may, however, have been born in one of the associated houses at the
back, when the whole group formed a single property in
the hands of Sir Thomas's father, Christopher Herbert the
younger (1583–1624). A passageway runs down through

the property to Lady Peckitt's Yard, named from the wife
of John Peckitt, Lord Mayor in 1701. It used to be the
custom of York that, while 'the mayor was a Lord for a year
and a day, his wife is a Lady for ever and aye'.

On the left are The Shambles and Colliergate, with a
narrow island block between, at the end of which is the little
garden with a parish hall, incorporating what is left of the
demolished church of St Crux, marking the principal cross-
roads of mediaeval York. The other arm of the transverse
road continues to the right as Fossgate and, after crossing
Foss Bridge, as Walmgate. We go on, but abandon the
recent Stonebow to the right and turn into St Saviourgate
past the old parish church on our right and the Centenary
Methodist Chapel on the left. Now wretchedly dwarfed by
the concrete car-park, church and chapel maintain their
dignity and may hope to outlast the brutalist bullyboy.
Beyond still stands one of the finest Georgian streets in York,
the south side largely built as a terrace about 1740. Houses
with known dates range from 1735 to 1780. On the left is
the cruciform Unitarian chapel of 1692. Bearing to the right
at the end of the street we pass the great bulk, now obscured
by newer buildings, of Peaseholme House, built in 1752 by
Robert Heworth, a carpenter turned builder, perhaps with
assistance from John Carr. We reach the new thoroughfare
of the Stonebow where it becomes Peaseholme Green. To
the left is St Anthony's Hall, now the Borthwick Institute;
to the right the Black Swan Inn. Beyond is St Cuthbert's
church, normally open, and with the unusual feature of
separate roofs of the same date, *c.* 1450, butted against one
another without a stone chancel arch or other mark of
division.

St Cuthbert's was saved in the sixteenth century by
personal intervention, as was St Martin in Micklegate. The
property where the Black Swan Inn now stands belonged to
the family of Bowes, who had been largely concerned in the

building during the fifteenth century. Sir Martin Bowes, Lord Mayor of London in 1545 and a wealthy goldsmith, interceded successfully for St Cuthbert's in 1547 and in recent years it has again been preserved from redundancy, this time by the devotion of the curate in charge, whose ministry has renewed parochial life. From St Anthony's Hall it is possible to reach the Minster by way of Aldwark and Ogleforth, or the centre of the city by Spen Lane and St Andrewgate. At present both routes are bordered by empty sites and dilapidation, but some few old buildings have been restored and others should be given a new lease of life by Lord Esher's plan.

Only one main route through historic York remains: that from north-west to east, from Bootham to Walmgate Bar. This starts as High Petergate, after the head of Stonegate becomes Low Petergate, then divides at King's Square into Colliergate and The Shambles and finally, as has been said, continues beyond Pavement as Fossgate and Walmgate. All the way was once a typical York mixture of high and low, with great mansions and in Walmgate even the palace of the Earls of Northumberland or Percy Inn, and Neville's Inn of the Earls of Westmorland. Now a great deal is run down, and most of old Walmgate has been demolished within the last twenty years. Only in Petergate are there still a few houses maintained at the highest level as professional premises, antique shops or offices, and the York College for Girls. What is left does manage to preserve, especially in Low Petergate and in The Shambles, the image of the Middle Ages in occasional glimpses rather than as a whole. It is a tragedy that so many mistaken permissions involving piece-meal destruction of the scene should have been given since the legislation of 1947, for this succession of streets was unique in England.

Just inside Bootham Bar on the left is a good house of 1782 in the style of the elder Peter Atkinson; a little further along on the other side No. 9 is timber-framed and belongs to a much older stratum of development. After crossing Duncombe Place before the west end of the Minster No. 23 on the right is a particularly fine brick house which belonged to the Vicars Choral and was completely rebuilt in 1780. On the left is the church of St Michael-le-Belfrey of 1525–37, designed by the Minster architect John Forman and an unusually noble example of late Tudor Gothic, before any trickle of the Renaissance appeared. The street continues largely Georgian, but the last house at the corner of Stonegate is of 1646. It was built in timber a year or more after it had been decreed that all houses 'be built upright from the ground in brick'. But here was St Peter's Liberty and exempt from civic control.

In the house on the other side of Stonegate, No. 51, lived Robert Ledger, a linen-draper and engraver, in 1755–63. Ledger, whose portrait is in the York Art Gallery, carried on a strangely mixed business. Not only did he engrave copper-plates and carry a 'large Assortment of all kinds of Linen-drapery Goods' but also 'Coffee, Tea, and Chocolate'. In 1763 he left York for London, where he had taken Symon's Wharf in Southwark, but recommended his brother-in-law Robert Holmes who continued the business at the Stonegate-Petergate corner, and introduced new lines: 'Holroyd's Billiard Sticks and Balls' and 'Neat Copper-plate Tables, the size of a small Pocket-Book, exhibiting the Rising of the Sun, calculated for the Meridian of York; also great Variety of Borderings for Pictures, with good Allowance to those who buy them to sell again'.

The first part of Low Petergate is Georgian, with several good houses and rather further on the notable York College for Girls in an early Georgian mansion, No. 62. Opposite to this, however, is the start of a range of much older jettied houses, timber-framed, with some of the most reliable old businesses in the city still occupying the shops: decorators, drapers, bakers, grocers, tailors, pork butchers, a butcher, a toyshop. Here, if anywhere, the spirit of old York lives on and through a narrow entry on the left we may enter Hornpot Lane and reach the church of Holy Trinity. Now redundant, the fabric has been taken over and beautifully repaired and refitted by the Redundant Churches Fund as a model of precisely what should be done. It is sad that the church no longer has a congregation, but it is a centre of affection for its body of Friends and for the traders of Goodramgate who over a period of years were instrumental in saving it. In this lovely little building and its calm churchyard, so well maintained, is the germ of a rejuvenated city of improved amenities. Along the Goodramgate frontage of the churchyard is a range of houses built in 1316 as a chantry investment and believed to be the oldest still occupied in York.

At the point where Petergate ends at Church Street and Goodramgate there opens King's Square. Until 1937 this was the site of the church of Holy Trinity in King's Court, apparently the palace precinct of the Viking Kings, on the north-east side of the street between the foot of Goodramgate and St Andrewgate, and just outside the gate of the Roman fortress. The townscape has lost greatly by the removal of the tiny church, which was a focal point, and also by the destruction of several of the good old houses which surrounded the 'square'. The highway continues as Colliergate, which still has a few interesting buildings, notably No. 19 of 1748. Parallel to Colliergate, bearing right out of King's Square, is the famous mediaeval street called The Shambles, from the many butchers' shops which formerly congregated there. Few are left now, and the jettied and gabled houses have mostly become shops for the sale of arts and crafts or tourist souvenirs, though in some genuine craftsmanship still continues. Through alleys and entries on the right are glimpses of the market, busiest on Friday and Saturday.

Fossgate, and its continuation Walmgate, have already

been mentioned, and now contain relatively little that is of passing interest. There are, however, one of the best preserved mediaeval buildings, the Hall of the Merchant Adventurers, and two churches, both normally closed. St Denys, Walmgate, on a slight eminence to the south of the street, has some of the finest glass and it is to be hoped that it may once more become accessible to regular visitors. St Margaret, mainly of interest for its setting and for the carved Norman porch, stands a short distance off the street in its own graveyard, now maintained by the local authority and a green island amid the desolation of slum clearance and redevelopment. Here we have come, facing Walmgate Bar, to the end of the road.

5 The Minster and the Close

In our perambulation we have several times passed close to York Minster and have touched its Close, but this great building and the complex which surrounds it cannot be dealt with in a casual manner. Besides the Close itself and the adjacent area of the old Liberty of St Peter we have to deal with the famous street of Stonegate, partly in the liberty, and with several lesser streets and lanes in the neighbourhood. Reversing the usual order of approach, which is to rush to the Minster and then explore the surroundings, we shall leave the principal matter to the end and first describe the setting. This can best be done by starting in Museum Street, where our earlier perambulation of the Walls entered the Museum Gardens opposite the end of Lendal.

To our left, behind the ruined St Leonard's Hospital, is the modern Public Library, housing the city archives and the early files of newspapers, magnificently indexed. Ahead are traffic lights with St Leonard's Place to left and Blake Street to right; before us is the wide area of Duncombe Place, a clearance of 1860–2 beside the ancient Lop Lane or Little Blake Street. From the lane there still survives the Red House of about 1722, in which lived Dr John Burton, Sterne's 'Dr Slop', for three years until he became involved in the Jacobite scare of 1745. Opposite to the Red House is the slanting entrance to Blake Street which runs southwards to St Helen's Square. On the right are the Assembly Rooms of 1731–6, designed by Lord Burlington in a very heavy copybook Palladian, relieved by the new front of 1828 added by J. P. Pritchett. In spite of their over-massive proportions, the Assembly Rooms make a good impression internally and the scene when costumes were to match must have been mighty fine. There are still a few old houses in the street, particularly No. 18 of 1789 by Peter Atkinson the elder, but a good deal of damage was done in the raid of 1942.

The church of St Helen was another saved in the sixteenth century by the activity of its parishioners. Much of it had actually been pulled down when they were able to obtain a private Act from Queen Mary, and re-erect it, but sometimes used bases for capitals and vice-versa. It was the parish church of the glass-painters who mostly lived in Stonegate, and the coat of arms assigned to the guild, showing the grozing irons and closing nails used, appears in the glass of the west window of the south aisle. Above the west gable is a small octagonal lantern, little more than a toy. This and one above the west front of St Michael-le-Belfrey were evidently based on the lantern of All Saints Pavement. Formerly the churchyard was to west of the church, but this produced an acute junction with Davygate, making it impossible for horse-drawn vehicles to turn from one street into the other. Accordingly in 1733 the bones were removed to a little space on the south-west side of Davygate, and the old graveyard became St Helen's Square.

Davygate, though it preserves the Christian name of David le Lardiner who lived in the early twelfth century, does not now contain much of historic concern. There was formerly an extra-parochial Liberty of Davy Hall, the prison of the King's Forest of Galtres in which the Lardiner family exercised hereditary jurisdiction, but it was ruinous by the fifteenth century. Eventually the site was bought by the corporation and in 1745–6 a row of houses called Cumberland Row, but now New Street, was put up by Charles Mitley, a carver, and the carpenter William Carr, whose home was on Bishophill. Mitley lived for a time in Marygate but when he died in 1758 was buried at St Cuthbert's. Though partially rebuilt in recent years, Cumberland Row still survives beside the new street which provides a short cut to Coney Street.

From St Helen's Square north-east to Minster Gates runs Stonegate, the most handsome street of the inner city and now wisely converted into a pedestrian precinct in which shoppers and gazers may wander at will. It is delightful to be able to stroll from side to side, to stand still at the best viewpoints, to take photographs, to sketch, without risk except from other passers-by. The volume of trade increases by leaps and bounds, disproving the often repeated nonsense that shoppers will not come where they cannot park a car. Here there is every inducement to stop and look, to browse, to delay departure to noisier and riskier places. Quite a high proportion of important shops are here, and there are also several alleyways and passages leading off Stonegate which add to its attractions.

The street rises slightly towards the Minster, but only about five feet in the whole length of Stonegate, some 200 yards. Starting at the bottom, the music shop on the corner of Blake Street is on the site of the house of Henry Hindley the celebrated clockmaker, later of Henry Sotheran the bookseller. Smeaton the engineer recorded Hindley's generosity to him when he was learning how to make philosophical instruments: 'my friend Hindley, from a principle the reverse of jealousy, communicated to me his method of division'. Hindley died aged 70 in 1771. The more interesting houses are mostly higher up, beyond the turning (to right) of Little Stonegate which leads to Back Swinegate and so to passages through into St Sampson's Square, the old Thursday Market. Unfortunately the alleys are now squalid rather than picturesque, but higher up is a parallel way called Coffee Yard between No. 31 and No. 33. Here is an intriguingly secret way between old houses, even passing through the screens passage of a forgotten mediaeval hall, half-way from Stonegate to Grape Lane.

It is not advisable to accept the dates marked on some of the old buildings of Stonegate, as at times they are the result of misreadings and misunderstandings. Little of what can now be seen from outside is strictly mediaeval, and the present building of Mulberry Hall, Nos. 17, 19, is really of 1574. The name is derived from the walled garden of the plot, already known as 'Mulberihawe' in 1361, evidence that the mulberry tree had been introduced two hundred years earlier than is generally believed (1548). This evidence comes from the will of John Alban, a York painter who wished to be buried in the nave of the Minster near the west door, which suggests that he may have been the designer of the great west window, painted in 1338 by Robert the 'verrour', probably Robert Ketelbarn, another inhabitant of Stonegate. Alban's own property was almost certainly No. 21, as it lay next to the entry (the passage to the York Medical Society at No. 23) of the property of the prior of St Oswald (of Nostell). Part of No. 23 goes back to 1590.

On the left of the street is a long passage leading back to the Star Inn, already famous in 1644 when its loyal landlord, William Foster, showed his displeasure at the arrival of victorious Roundheads as customers. 'Over against the Starre' on the right-hand side of Stonegate was the sign of the Bible, now No. 35, one of the most famous of book-seller's shops from 1682 to 1873. More recently it was the home and shop of the York glass-painter John W. Knowles and his son, the late John A. Knowles, antiquary and local historian. This is one of the mediaeval houses, going back to 1487, and with Nos. 37 and 39 formed the prebendal property of North Newbald held by Laurence Sterne from 1742. From a date formerly on the plaster, No. 37 was built or altered in 1677. The oldest house, not only in Stonegate but in York, is now a ruin, approached along the passageway beyond No. 50 on the left. It is a large late Norman building of the twelfth century and may well have been the prebendal house of Osbaldwick.

Stonegate ends at Petergate, but we cross over into Minster Gates, an oblique continuation aiming for the great south door of the Minster. This was formerly Low Minster Gates in contradistinction to the High Gates at the end of Lop Lane, giving admission to the area outside the west front. Low Minster Gates used also to be called Bookland Lane or Bookbinders' Alley, and its shops have often been connected with various aspects of the book trade and with stationery and the like requirements of the clerics attached to the cathedral. This entry to the Close has always been reserved for pedestrians by a row of posts or 'stulpes', mentioned as far back as 1370. So it is possible to stand here and gaze at the south front looming above the scene, with the great doorway built in time for the arrival of Henry III on his visit of 1244, when he had given orders in advance that wax tapers should be placed around the church and about St William's shrine.

We are now separated from the Minster by the traffic-ridden thoroughfare of Deangate, mistakenly permitted in the early years of this century. It is now not merely a desecration of the Close but the constant vibration is a cause of grave danger to the cathedral fabric as to all other neighbouring buildings. It divides the Minster from its attendant church of St Michael-le-Belfrey and splits the houses of Minster Yard into two parts. As things are, we must be content to circulate clockwise around the Minster, examin-

17　Top left *The tower of St Mary, Bishophill Junior, with a Saxon base of the tenth century and Norman upper stages;* 18 right *All Saints, North Street, with its steeple of* c. 1450, *imitating that of the neighbouring Blackfriars, now gone.*

19　Above *All Saints, Pavement. In the open lantern a light is said to have been set to guide benighted travellers through the Forest of Galtres.*

20 Above *The main front of York's Guildhall, designed by Robert Couper in 1447.*

21 Below *The interior of the timbered hall of the Merchant Adventurers.*

ing all the subsidiary buildings before approaching the architectural culmination of York. The first visit is to the church of St Michael-le-Belfrey, named it would seem from having been beside a detached bell-tower long ago destroyed, but represented by a turret (removed in 1872) on top of the gable of the south transept. The old church, replaced by this one in 1525, had been in poor repair and was continually being presented at visitations without result. What is remarkable at such a late date is the purity of Gothic style and excellently proportioned detail. Built all at one time, and even preserving much of its original stained glass, this must be considered the finest parish church of the reign of Henry VIII, anywhere in the country.

Crossing Deangate and passing in front of the west end of the Minster we enter the narrow lane of Precentor's Court, with Fenton House of 1680 facing us at the far end. To the right is No. 10, an ancient house with a Georgian front. Returning towards the Minster we turn to the left into the Dean's Park and pass by the railings of the Purey-Cust Chambers to reach the mouldering twelfth-century arches which are all that is left of the great hall (122 feet long by 76 feet broad) of the Archbishop's Palace. In front of us is the Chapel, converted into the Minster Library and much restored, but preserving the design of around 1230. This is late for its transitional style, with lancet windows combined with large semicircular arches. These scanty remnants remind us of the big rambling palace abandoned by the archbishops after they went out to Bishopthorpe, but used by visiting royalty and in the end leased to Sir Arthur Ingram, who made gardens and fishponds regarded as a Paradise by travellers of the 1630s.

Sir William Brereton, Bart, who was here in June 1635, wrote of the 'brave garden, whereof not a third part furnished with flowers, but disposed into little beds, whereon placed statues; the beds all grass . . . large fair trees . . . a spacious

orchard wherein are many walks'. The previous year
Lieutenant Hammond had seen 'adioyning to the Minster a
second Paradice . . . The first moyitie of an houre, wee spent
in his (Sir Arthur Ingram's) rare Gardens, and curious long
walkes, which were adorn'd with many kinds of Beasts to the
Life, with most liuely Statues in seuerall shapes and formes.
A pleasant fayre Tennis Court; a delightful large bowling
ground, newlie made; curiously contriu'd Fish-Ponds . . .
A place it is so pleasant to all the sences as Nature and Art
can make it.' William Drew, Sir Arthur's gardener, had 50s
a quarter for 'keeping and weedinge the Garden orchard &
highe walke . . . kitchine Garden, and alsoe for keeping the
fish ponnds & . . . keepinge ye Connys' (rabbits).

Although the statues and figures of beasts have gone, the
park still has beautiful trees and green grass, and there are
plenty of roses and other flowers in the gardens of the
Deanery and the canons' houses. A footpath takes us behind
the Chapter House to the front of the Treasurer's House,
which belongs to the National Trust and is open to the
public every day except Good Friday from April to the end
of October. As was mentioned during the circuit of the
Walls, much of the mediaeval Treasurer's House is in the
adjoining Gray's Court. What is here accessible is very
largely a building of about 1700, extremely fine in quality
and containing good fittings and a notable collection of
furniture.

Past Chapter House Street, which leads to the entrance of
Gray's Court and to Ogleforth which runs to Goodramgate
and Monk Bar, we pass several small eighteenth-century
houses of Minster Yard to reach College Street. Here on our
left is St William's College, now extensively restored but
preserving much of the original courtyard house of the later
fifteenth century, with additions made two hundred years
later. This was a college of chantry priests, but there was a
much earlier college of the Vicars Choral who took services

on behalf of the canons. The college of Vicars was housed in
the Bedern, beyond Goodramgate and in a separate part of
St Peter's Liberty approached by a bridge over the street.
The bridge is no longer there, and we have to leave the Close
by its last remaining gate, next to the office of the National
Trust, cross the street, and slightly to the left pass through
the entry between Nos. 25 and 27. The courtyard of the
Bedern is now a melancholy sight, and all that remains of
the Middle Ages consists of the lower part of the walls of the
Chapel of 1348, on our right. The lack of care that led to the
destruction of this historic and beautiful little building is a
sad commentary upon the insensitive world in which we live.

We return to College Street with a magnificent view of the
east front of the Minster ahead, over the new and pleasing
layout of College Green. Bearing left we pass the Old
Residence, believed to have been built in 1727 by Samuel
Sidall or Sydal, a local carpenter and builder; it now forms
the junior school of the York College for Girls. On our right
are good views of the changing detail of the Minster: the
east end of 1361–73, the eastern transepts and western bays
of the choir, of *c.* 1385–1400, the Zouche Chapel and
vestries begun in 1350 nestling under the south side of the
choir; and the east side of the great South Transept of about
1230–41. It is the great transept that is the earliest part of
the present Minster, barring mere fragments and foundations, and represents the start of a new Gothic cathedral.
Like a magnified shrine the transept lies on a north–south
axis, athwart the orientation of the church. It is reasonable to
suppose that it was actually designed as an outer shrine
within which the shrine of St William of York might be
fittingly housed.

Before entering the Minster by the south door it is time
to take stock of the historical background that led to the
building of the cathedral as we know it. That it is possible to
do this is due to the archaeological discoveries during the

excavations since 1966. We now know that the enormous size of the church is controlled by certain dimensions of its Norman predecessor. The position and size of the central crossing with its tower; the unusual width of the nave; the overall length of the nave and the west front with two towers; the length of the great transept from north to south — all these are derived from the original Norman work of Archbishop Thomas of Bayeux begun in 1080 and from additions to it made before the end of the twelfth century. Something has already been said (above, p. 26) of this earlier cathedral, and we may visit the interior of its successor.

Once inside the south door we face the Five Sisters window at the north end of the transept, surmounted in the gable beneath the wooden vault by another five smaller lancets, graduated. The five tall lancets are all of the same height and retain their grizzale glass contemporary with the completion of the building, about 1250. They are 53 feet high and five feet wide, containing between them over 1300 square feet of glass. Since York Minster actually preserves panels of glass of a much earlier date, c. 1150, with figures and in full colour, it is an interesting question just why the grand new Gothic transept should have adopted geometrical patterns almost without colour. The answer is to be found by considering the architectural character of the building.

We must remember first of all that York was, like many others, a great church of royal foundation. Its works were likely to attract the interest of the Crown, and we know that this was in fact the case here. Henry III was personally interested in the new transept, and his taste counted for a great deal. Whether he sent a master mason to give advice is unknown, but we may assume a benevolent concern from the start. Secondly, there is the precise relationship of the style to other works in the North. Dr Gee has shown that the closest links, both of style and of working masons (indicated by the same marks) are with the great abbeys of Rievaulx,

Fountains (eastern transept), Byland, and Roche, places where the relevant phases of work were in progress during the generation roughly 1210–40, while the date of the York transept is perhaps 1225–50. The abbeys named were all Cistercian: they were forbidden by the rule to use coloured glass. The king too was closely concerned with Cistercian building, at Waverley in Surrey, at Hayles in Gloucestershire, at Netley in Hampshire. One of the architectural masters who had charge of the king's works was the Cistercian lay-brother and mason, John of Waverley.

It is probably significant too that Salisbury Cathedral, also begun in 1220 and under the patronage of Henry III who spent much of his time at Clarendon a few miles away, was glazed with grizzale. There too were tall lancets, the use of slender shafts of dark marble, a restrained and almost puritan aesthetic. Though York and Salisbury differ greatly in their individual designs, they share this particular feeling of the period, a strict control of line and form within the Early English style. In looking at the York transept we must bear in mind, too, that the crossing has been greatly altered. The Norman tower was rebuilt in a form probably rather like that of the lower stage of the Lincoln central tower – which indeed may have been a slightly later copy on a smaller scale. From fragments discovered in the excavations we know that the crossing piers of the tower of *c.* 1230–50 had marble shafting, and the piers were relatively slender. This accounted for the grave distortions of the building, due to the sway of the thirteenth-century tower under wind pressure, long before that tower fell in 1407. So the whole transept, as it was when first finished, would have looked all of a piece, trim, sharp, and neat, lit palely through the tall lancets with shafts of light bringing out the pallor of the Magnesian limestone.

The two arms of the transept are not of identical design. This is certainly connected with the different sources of finance responsible: the north transept and the crossing and tower were paid for by Canon John Romanus, the sub-dean and later treasurer, who had completed them before he died in 1255. The south transept, on the other hand, was the responsibility of the chapter, greatly helped by Archbishop Gray, who had his own chantry and tomb prepared in the central chapel on the east side. The contemporary shrine of St William, which must have been costly, probably stood in the south transept, and this would have been at the expense of the chapter, thus equalising matters. Despite the differences of detail, and the slightly earlier character of Romanus's work in the northern arm, the transept 'read' as a whole, and notwithstanding the changes still does. We are seeing basically what King Henry saw when he came in this same doorway in the summer of 1244.

We do not know if the lantern of the old tower let light into the crossing in the way its successor does; if not, the look of the grand new building must have been altogether more sombre, though the Five Sisters were not obscured by time – if, indeed, they were already glazed. The timber vaults were not the same, but they were of wood, painted to look like stone, a treatment ordered by Henry III for his chapel at Windsor after he had seen the new wooden vaults at Lichfield in 1243, the year before his state visit to York. We even know the name of the master carpenter who was in charge of making at least part of these roofs and vaults: Gilbert of Corbridge, son of William the carpenter, rewarded by Archbishop Gray in 1226 and in 1248, when he was said to have been long in the archbishop's service and to have worked well both at Bishopthorpe and on the Minster. Before leaving the transept with a last glance at the Five Sisters, it is satisfying to note that, 50 years ago, their glass was releaded largely with pigs of mediaeval lead melted down by the commissioners of Henry VIII from the roofs of the Cistercian abbey at Rievaulx; the pigs were buried under a

fall of masonry undermined too soon, to be found by ex-
cavation after the abbey ruins were taken over by H.M.
Office of Works. Poetic justice is seldom so neat.

From the transept it is logical to continue through it to
its splendid annexe, the Chapter House. This, like those at
Lincoln, Westminster, and Salisbury, is a polygon, but unlike them has no central pillar and its vault is of timber, held
up by a remarkable trussed timber roof. Some of the masons
who had worked on the north transept moved on to the
chapter house, at first built on its own and only later connected by the L-shaped vestibule that we now pass through
to reach it. As was the case at Wells, there was a long delay
between the start and finish of the work. Probably the
changes in design were due to elimination of a central pillar
originally planned. At any rate, the building was not
finished until the 1280s, nor the vestibule until 1290. Here
we may disregard the more minute details of style and consider simply the aesthetic impact of a very remarkable work
of major architecture. The tall, stone-vaulted vestibule leads
us, by surprise as it were, through a right-angle and to the
chapter-house doors, covered with some of the finest
patterned wrought iron of the thirteenth century.

Let us set aside all quibbles about forms of construction
and admire our greatest mediaeval dome. For the wooden
vault, suspended as it is from the pyramidal roof above, is a
visual dome or firmament fit to set beside those of the East.
The windows, of pure geometrical tracery, have been carried
to the limits of size and through their patterns and armorials
pours a flood of light. Aeneas Sylvius Piccolomini, later
Pope Pius II, riding incognito through York in 1435,
remarked on two things only, that it was a large and populous
city, and that the cathedral, notable in the whole world for
its size and architecture, had 'a very brilliant chapel whose
glass walls are held together by very slender columns'. That
is the essence of the York chapter-house, even though it is

not a chapel. A glass chapel, almost it might be thought 'a sunny pleasure-dome with caves of ice', forgetting the practical purpose of its arcaded seats beneath the glazing, used now for almost 700 years for the quarterly meetings of the dean and chapter. Yet surely its moment of glory came when King Richard II sat there in state on Thursday 1 June 1396, the feast of Corpus Christi, and a long bench had been provided for 'the Mayor and aldermen of the city in the chapter house of the greater church of St Peter of York'.

Built in the heyday of Edward I, our greatest king; used and dignified by the most art-loving, Richard II; described by the famous tag: *Ut rosa flos florum, sic est domus ista domorum* – 'the chief of houses, as of flowers the rose is', the York chapter-house has ever been – and may it long remain – a unique experience. After it the other beauties of the Minster are in some sense an anticlimax. Bursting their way through the centre of the old round-arched church Archbishop Gray and Canon Romanus – in the rest of his life a notorious miser and skinflint, a profiteering pluralist and cranky to boot – had achieved their end. Around the shrine of St William had been placed an architectural outer shell original in design but following the best patterns of the day. To this their successors had added, as a necessary boardroom for the directors of the church, a transparent capsule of unparalleled magnificence. What was left? To rebuild the cathedral, nothing more.

Until now we have progressed up the map, making towards the Chapter House as our Pole. Like all polar explorers we are left with nothing to do but retrace our steps. In a second pilgrimage we have to seek the East, the sunrise of the Sun of Righteousness, following the chronology of the new Gothic church which, more or less, was built from west to east and then back to the centre to aim for heaven with the central tower. First, to rinse our minds from the magnetic attraction to which they have been subjected, let us stroll around the whole of the outside, and round again until we reach the west doors. The shrine and the dome lie at the end of Stonegate and Minster Gates, forming a triumphal way though not in one straight line towards the royal portal. The west front, though it can be seen rising majestically above the roofs of the city from the other side of the river, has no such logical approach. There is no transition, no link such as that of Minster Gates; whether we come from Duncombe Place or from Bootham Bar, the front is askew, off centre. Perhaps this is just as well, lending an unexpected attraction, a discord left unresolved from without.

Seen at close quarters the front is not an aesthetic success. The bits and pieces of different dates and by several schemes of successive architects are manifest and not altogether compatible. Useful as a copybook of Gothic style: the Geometrical ground stage, Curvilinear upper windows, ogee tracery above the earlier central door and even, as remarked by Dr Gee, the single use of ball-flower ornament in the little gable above, the Perpendicular towers, the west end of York fails to cohere. Once past the doorways it is another story. The nave from within is, in its own way, a masterpiece. Most of it was built in a single generation, from 1291 to 1322, and probably throughout under Simon of York as chief architect. The wooden vault of the high span, now a replica after the fire of 1840, was not finished until *c.* 1360. The patterned vault, imitating the masonry vaults of its own time, is much like those of the mid-fourteenth century at Gloucester, Tewkesbury, Pershore, and the new choir of Ely. It could only be of timber, notwithstanding the flying buttresses provided, because of the inordinate span of 45 feet, forced on Master Simon by the foundations of the Norman nave.

It is Simon's design, the outcome of native tradition fertilised by up-to-date knowledge of what was happening in

France, and specifically in Troyes the capital of Champagne, that is pacemaking. Here is verticality shown by the prominent vaulting shafts within the piers, fully integrated with a triforium and clerestory combined as one pattern, and lightly drawn together from end to end by the horizontal line of the stringcourse above the main arches. We look eastwards, glimpsing the top of the east window above the organ, mounted on the asymmetrical rood-screen or pulpitum. Beneath the arcades we can see the stone vaults of the aisles, and passing through into them, study at leisure their noble array of glass. The two easternmost windows, of north and south aisles, are the earliest in England, probably in Europe, to have made effective artistic use of the new process of yellow stain. The rediscovery of this chemical trick, firing in a kiln pieces of white glass painted with silver salts or with finely ground filings, was due to King Alfonso the Wise of Castile, brother-in-law of Edward 1. He brought together the scientists of his time and a body of learned translators from Arabic and Hebrew, who by 1279 produced a compendium of chemical knowledge including the vital secret of the exquisite golden glass of the hanging lamps of the East. King Alfonso and Edward 1 both employed, at this very time, the same English clerk, Geoffrey of Eversley, and it may well have been through him or his diplomatic bag that the secret reached us. Probably it was once more due to the royal patronage of York Minster that the first use of it was made at York before 1310.

The great west window and its glass are later. They form part of the campaign led by Archbishop William Melton to complete the great churches of his diocese and province. Once again the hour produced the man, the archbishop's architect Ivo de Raghton. Master Ivo came from the old family of hereditary falconers who kept the King's hawks within the Forest of Carlisle, and settled in York early in his career. He designed the east window at Carlisle Cathedral as well as the west window at York, and was the inventive genius behind the richly flowing Curvilinear style of northern England – the style which so captured the fancy of foreign masons that they carried it to Flanders and Germany and developed it into what is called Flamboyant. In England it was soon superseded by the rigid Perpendicular, but abroad it spread and burgeoned until by the sixteenth century it had reached Spain and Portugal, Italy, Poland, and at last France. Ivo's great window was filled by the glass painted in 1338 by Robert the glazier and perhaps designed by John Alban, whose grave is beneath our feet.

Shortly before the appalling epidemic of plague, the Black Death, struck in 1348, the next stage had been planned: an enlarged Gothic choir was to take the place of the twelfth-century work of Archbishop Roger. To maintain the old choir in use for as long as possible, the new east end, a Lady Chapel, was to be built outside it and further to the east. Yet, because of the existence of the old parish church of St Mary ad Valvas, 'at the Gates', it was necessary to curtail the last bay which, as we can see, is narrower than the standard width that rules the rest of the nave and choir. This Lady Chapel was also under the special patronage of an archbishop, John Thoresby, and the four easternmost bays were built in the twelve years from 1361 to 1373, when he died. Funds ran short, and it was not until after 1385 that the western bays, to contain the stalls of the choir, were begun. So it is that we find the personal styles of at least three different architects: William Hoton, Robert Patrington, and Hugh Hedon, between the central tower and the east front. A fourth style, earlier than any of those and perhaps that of Hoton's father of the same name who died in 1351, is displayed in the charming chantry chapel of Archbishop Zouche south of the choir, now reserved for private prayer.

The individual styles play, as variations on a theme, upon

the basic design set forth in the nave of 1291. In spite of the Perpendicular detail which reigned after 1350, the whole Minster from west to east is internally a single recognisable whole. Above the vestibule to the Chapter House a drawing office for the master mason was built by the middle of the fourteenth century. There, on a flat floor-slab of plaster, the master and his assistants set out to full size the details of the work; and there must have been preserved, finely drawn in ink on great skins of parchment, the original drawings of Master Simon and the versions produced by his successors. None of these drawings have survived, except those on the plaster floor, but at Strasburg and Vienna may still be seen collections of drawings, built up over the centuries, to show how the mediaeval cathedrals were designed and built.

The greatest thing in the Minster is its astonishing wealth of stained glass. Used as we are to the almost universal destruction of this fragile material at the hands of the puritans and Parliamentarian soldiery, it comes as a surprise that the personal authority of one man, Ferdinando Lord Fairfax, should have been able to save what is here. Ten generations of Englishmen, and of foreign travellers, owe the wonder of this treasury of colour to his intervention on behalf of the honour and the glory of Yorkshire and its capital. Many of us deplore his politics, but all must acclaim his firm stand on behalf of law and order in the midst of war, and for the preservation of beauty above all. It is impossible here to discuss the detail, window by window, and it must suffice that we stand or sit beyond the sanctuary to gaze at the magnificent expanse of the great east window. Painted in 1405–8 by John Thornton from Coventry, who fulfilled his contract to complete the job in three years, it is by far the most remarkable work of its kind in England. We look, we marvel, and we leave it reluctant and thoughtful.

After the Chapter House, the cathedral was an anti-climax; likewise anything else after the east window. Yet

in its completion the Minster attained another peak: the
central lantern. Attempts to underpin and preserve the old
central tower, 'lofty and delectable to see', begun with funds
given by Richard II in 1395, were defeated by its fall in
1407. It was brought down by a great storm combined with
'the carelessness of the masons'. King Henry IV, as royal
patron, sent Master William Colchester from Westminster
Abbey to York and old Hugh Hedon, disgraced, died
within the year. Colchester and his southern assistant were
set upon and nearly murdered by the York masons, but in
the long run their skill prevailed. Competent as an engineer,
Colchester stiffened the eastern piers of the crossing with
stone screens, rebuilt a weak column in the north transept,
solidified the western piers and their abutments. He died in
1420, believing that upon this solid basis there would be
erected the greatest tower in England: not just the giant
lantern we see, but also a higher bell-chamber above it, and
even a tall spire to outdo those of Lincoln and Old St Paul's.
His successors took fright and left the tower unfinished,
chopped off as it is. The south-west tower was added for the
ring of bells, and the north-west for symmetry. Colchester's
scheme for the rood-screen which, as royal architect, he had
designed to bear statues of the fourteen kings from William
the Conqueror to his sovereign, Henry V, seven each side of
the doorway, was squeezed sideways to fit in Henry VI as the
fifteenth. It was almost certainly finished under the Dean,
Richard Andrew, who was also secretary to Henry VI from
1443 to 1455.

There remained to do the windows and vaulting of the
lantern, all that was to be completed of Colchester's central
project. After the civil tumult of the Wars of the Roses had
died down a fresh start was made. Carvers were set to work
on the wooden vaulting and bosses in 1471, and the iron
bars and glass were inserted in the tall windows. A rich
colour scheme was added by the painters in the following

year and from the accounts we know their palette: verdigris, indigo, vermilion, red lead, ochre, and white lead, together with linseed oil, varnish, and mastic. The Minster was reckoned as complete and on 3 July 1472 the service of consecration was held at last. The archbishop was George Neville, Andrew was still dean; the master mason Robert Spillesby, who had only a few more months to live; the chief carpenter John Forster; James Dam and David Dam were the carvers; Matthew Petty the glazier – the tip of a submerged iceberg, token of the multitude of prelates, clerks, craftsmen, labourers, pilgrims, penitents, contributors to the Minster.

6 *Mediaeval York*

Now that we have seen the city as it is we can consider how York became its present self. The site and a ghost of the defences of the Roman settlement survived the floods and the Dark Age, as we saw, but from the first York which Alcuin knew to the consummation of the Minster we see, seven centuries were to elapse: as long after Alcuin's time as his was from the founding of the Roman fortress of Eboracum. Of the first three of those seven hundred years we know very little, and what we do know is mainly the result of quite recent archaeological research, dovetailed into the few dates provided by chronicles and the background of social life implied by literary sources. York begins to take shape after it had been occupied by the Danes in 867 and had become the capital of a Viking kingdom under Halfdan in 875. This independent kingdom lasted until 954, but right up to the Norman Conquest York remained very closely tied to the Scandinavian world and was happy to form part of the northern empire of Sweyn and Canute after 1014. There were also relations with the parallel Viking kingdom of Dublin, and the old route by sea and land, up the river to York and then through the Pennines to the Irish sea, was again thronged.

Putting together the scraps of information from various sources to give a picture of Viking York, two main facets of its history emerge. The first is that the outlines of the mediaeval and modern street plan had already been formed, conditioned by the new crossing of the river at or near Ouse Bridge; and that the town was thickly populated. Along the streets were closely packed small houses of timber, of no architectural pretensions and comparatively short life. Secondly, the place had high economic and social standards for its period, though that may not be saying much. There is evidence of working both iron and bronze and of a large leather industry. Bone was used for making combs, pins, and many other minor objects of necessity and luxury. There were the purely luxury trades of manufacturing beads of glass and from amber, and flutes were cut from hollow bones and from wood. In winter a favourite recreation must have been skating on the ice, for skates of bone, well worn, are numerous. Great quantities of meat were eaten, largely beef and venison, but also mutton and pork, as well as poultry. The importation of fish was, of course, a major business, and oysters and mussels were included in the diet. Cereals were grown in the surrounding villages and a good deal of fruit and nuts were eaten. The fruit found include both the sloe and a cultivated plum, and what may have been a damson; hazel nuts were abundant, and there are signs that flax, hops, spinach, and cabbage were cultivated. The weeds include a number of herbs which may have been grown for their medical value: sorrel, chickweed, nettle, mugwort, groundsel, poppy, and devil's bit scabious. The diminutive flax *Linum catharticum* was probably in use as a yellow dye-stuff. Many other plants have been identified from their pollen and it is possible that the list of herbs deliberately cultivated should be extended.

The development of the street plan is largely a matter for surmise, though later documentary evidence can in some

22. *St Leonard's Place, built in 1834–5 to the designs of the younger Peter Atkinson. On the left is the new front added to the Assembly Rooms in 1828 to the design of James Pritchett.*

23 Top *The Assize Courts, designed by John Carr in 1765 and built in 1773-7.*
24 Above *Inside Lord Burlington's Assembly Rooms of 1731-6.*

cases be legitimately projected back to the pre-Conquest period. Outside the remains of the fortress area the principal feature was the cross-roads formed by two wide swathes of land which intersected at the site of the later church of St Crux. From the south-east gate of the old fortress, beside the Viking King's palace or court, one wide street settlement ran down towards the Foss. The outer limits of this can be identified as the east side of Colliergate and west side of the Shambles, leaving an open green or market place between them. Only much later was this built up with a middle row. Beyond the intersection these lines continue as the east side of Fossgate and the west side of the lane leading past Lady Peckitt's Yard to the edge of the Foss. The other road started opposite to Micklegate at the eastern end of the ford or bridge and climbed the river bank between the north side of the water lane beyond St Michael's churchyard, and the south side of what was later known as First Water Lane and is now King Street.

Higher up the line of this green or droveway extended from the south side of Coppergate, Pavement and the old Stonebow Lane, continuing to Peaseholme Green, as far north as the north side of the branch of Peter Lane Little on which the church stood, an alleyway which for several centuries ran through the block to The Shambles, and so to the north side of St Saviourgate. The positions of the mediaeval churches become more intelligible. As has been noted, there were at least 39 parish churches by 1137, practically all those known. Of them no fewer than eight were in this 'green belt': St Michael, Spurriergate; St Peter the Little; All Saints, Pavement; St Crux; Christ Church in King's Court; St Saviour; All Saints, Peaseholme Green; and St Cuthbert. All these could have been founded on open ground in churchyards formed from the green. The building up of middle rows and of closely planted blocks came later but, as proved by the devastating spread of the fire in 1137, by early in the twelfth century. It is worth noting that the line of streets outside the south-east wall of the Roman fortress: Jubbergate, Newgate, St Andrewgate, must have been formed earlier, and built up further out to the old edge of the green ways.

There is in fact good reason for thinking that York was already a widespread city well before the Conquest. There has been a persistent tendency to underestimate the mediaeval population, over-reacting against the statements of early writers. In the Life of St Oswald it is said that about AD 1000 there were 30,000 adults in York, which would imply a total population of the order of 45,000. Is this credible? Yes, on one condition: that we admit that the city was a 'Greater York' and included that area of 84 carucates which at the Domesday Survey gelded with the city, and was presumably the same as that which the Danish settlers had been said to cultivate 'round about'. Definite figures for the number of houses are given in Domesday, referring to 1065 in King Edward's time. There were 1,607 *mansiones* in six of the seven shires or wards of the city, but to this must be added one shire taken for building the two castles, and the fee of St Mary's Abbey, omitted by the compilers. In the city and its immediate suburbs the total must have been about 2,000; but a *mansio* was more than a single house. It was rather the toft or large plot on which the tax of house-gavel was paid, and might contain several households.

Long afterwards, about 1639, a count was made showing 1,786 houses within the walls and 370 in the suburbs; while in 1672 the hearth tax shows 2,124 households in all. The population of 1672, estimated from other sources, suggests that an average of between $5\frac{1}{2}$ and 6 persons lived in every house. Finally we reach the fairly accurate figures of the census of 1801, when the total for the city with its liberties (but not Marygate) was 16,846; and that for Marygate and the whole ring of outer parishes which probably constituted

the 84 carucates was 4,009, giving a combined total of
20,855. It may seem *prima facie* unlikely that numbers at the
opening of the nineteenth century should have been less than
half what they were at the end of the Dark Ages, but against
this we must set two major factors. York in AD 1000 was
effectively the capital of a large kingdom and also a first-
class seaport trading with all Northern Europe. In 1800
York was notoriously an impoverished and effete county
town, coming seventeenth on the list of English cities after
London. It had long before been overtaken by Norwich and
Bristol, but now its 16,000 inhabitants were outstripped in
Yorkshire alone by the 53,000 of Leeds, the 31,000 of
Sheffield, and the 29,000 of Hull.

After the Conquest, and the deliberate 'harrying of the
North' in 1069–70, it is notorious that the amount of waste
– that is, settlement worth nothing – was outstandingly high
in Yorkshire. The reason for a catastrophic drop in population is not far to seek, and the abandonment of the city by
many Scandinavian traders will account for the rest. York
completely lost its sovereign status, and had to struggle
through the ups and downs of many centuries, fires, plagues,
and the loss of trade to more active or better placed rivals. By
the time the stone walls came to be built, between 1250 and
1350, they left outside large areas which had certainly been
considered parts of York at the Conquest, and probably
earlier. Some of these outer districts had been given to St
Mary's Abbey, but many belonged to the archbishop and
are listed in documents of 1080 and 1106 setting out his
privileges: Layerthorpe, Monkgate, Walmgate beyond
Thurbrand's house, all Clementhorpe and (the parish of) St
Mary (Bishophill Junior), with the third penny of what
comes in Walmgate and Fishergate and the Fish Market on
the Foss. The archbishop also took the whole of the tolls on
ships mooring at Clementhorpe and as far down river as the
archbishop's fee extends. This placed the most important

part of the harbour in the archbishop's hands, with the later shipbuilding yards; and he also had the valuable tolls of all merchants who passed through Micklegate Bar or stopped there.

What did not belong to St Peter's and the archbishop, or to St Mary's Abbey, was largely in the hands of other religious houses: Holy Trinity Priory and its extensive jurisdiction outside the city to the south-west; St Clement's nunnery in Clementhorpe; St Andrew's Priory in Fishergate; the great Hospital; and scattered properties and rights given to the Church of Durham and others. After 1227 large areas of land in the city were set aside for the orders of friars: the Black Friars, Grey Friars, Carmelites, and Austin Friars, and until they were extinguished in 1310, also the Friars of the Sack. All this meant that mediaeval York was a jigsaw of pieces divided by mostly invisible lines, or by precinct walls. Rents, taxes, and rates were paid to different lords and in different proportions. The constables of the city might have jurisdiction on one side of the street, as in Bootham, or half-way up, as in Stonegate; but were inhibited beyond the centre of the highway or a mark set in the wall. The exempt jurisdictions, liberties, and extra-parochial areas tended to become inhabited by those who could not afford to pay the city's heavy dues or to buy the freedom which was essential to carry on any trade or occupation in the city proper (p. 117). As time went on the disproportion of wealth became more and more marked, and the paupers in some of the exempt parishes might greatly exceed those who could pay rates. Thus in 1632, when assessments survive for the whole of York, Bishophill Junior had 26 poor to 4 rate-payers; St Olave Marygate had 25 poor to 11; whereas St Martin Coney Street had only 3 paupers to 41 and All Saints Pavement 2 to 31 paying.

The division and subdivision of property and rights were almost infinitely complex. Besides the great fees of the king

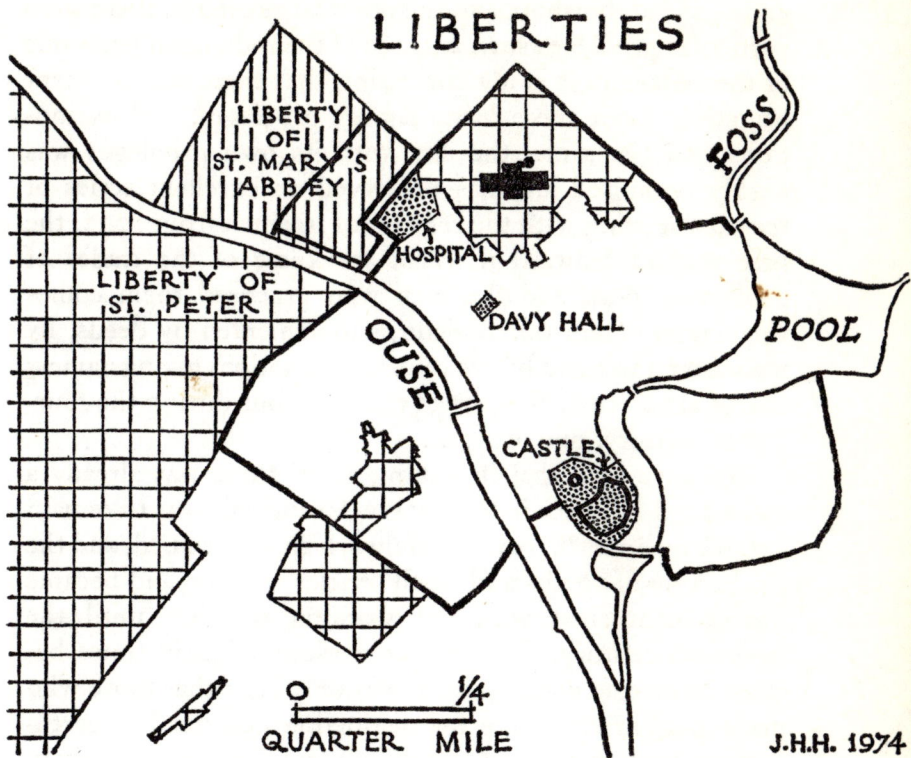

LIBERTIES

LIBERTY OF ST. MARY'S ABBEY

LIBERTY OF ST. PETER

FOSS

HOSPITAL

DAVY HALL

OUSE

POOL

CASTLE

QUARTER MILE

J.H.H. 1974

York in the Middle Ages was made up of many different jurisdictions, each
under its own local authority. Besides the area controlled by the
Corporation (the Mayor and Citizens) there were completely independent
liberties belonging to the Dean and Chapter of the Minister (the Liberty
of St Peter); the Abbot and Convent of St Mary (St Mary's Liberty,
including both the abbey precinct and the hamlet of Marygate); the great
Hospital of St Peter and St Leonard; the King's Forester at Davy Hall;
and the royal precinct of York Castle. All of these had their own courts,
their own police, and their own prisons.

and of the archbishop, and the other large estates, there were particular privileges such as those of the individual prebends of the Minster. It is not surprising that there was frequent litigation about these many rights, privileges, and exemptions. All the same, the city with its own privileges was highly organised and has preserved an excellent series of records, starting with the register of freemen from 1272, the first year of Edward I. What we know of the trades of mediaeval York and the men who practised them comes very largely from this register, supplemented by deeds, by wills after 1321 and by the returns of taxations giving names: one of about 1282 for part of the city, four during the fourteenth century, one of 1524.

We have seen that in Viking times there was already a substantial industry in leather goods, and this was to remain a staple business in York. Metalwork also continued, and the production of combs and small articles went on and became mainly concerned with the working of horn until the twentieth century. The bronze workers of early times became known as potters and it was only later that those who made pots in clay were for distinction described as earthpotters. Potters were often bellfounders, but dealt mainly in household and kitchen vessels, pots, pans, skillets, saucepans, flagons, and the like. From the Poll Taxes of 1377 and 1381, which have been printed, it is possible to get a good idea of the population and what was going on in the different parishes. The recorded names, certainly fewer than the real total, amounted to 7,250 inhabitants over 14 within inner York; this must mean a complete population there of at least 11,000. In 1396 Richard II gave alms to 12,040 poor persons at York, and such a figure implies that greater York can hardly have had fewer than 15,000 in all.

Out of these about a thousand can be identified by occupation and allocated to their trades. There were roughly 100 different crafts, and of the 1,000 identifiable individuals about 100 were middlemen, and 50 were professional. The proportion of men engaged simply in buying and selling, the merchant and shopkeeper class, was on the increase, and before the middle of the fifteenth century was in control of the city government. This is hardly surprising, for in a list of over 100 English towns and the things for which they were famous, compiled soon after 1300, York was named second and renowned for its 'regraterie', i.e. retail trade. Though some of the characteristics named are obvious, such as the School of Oxford, the Plains of Salisbury, the Marvel of Stonehenge, and the Baths of Bath, it is curious to find that Winchester was considered primarily famous for its Butchers, Norwich for its Haven, Grantham for Thieves, or Shrewsbury for Pilgrims.

The first freeman of York on the roll is Thomas de Fulford, a cordwainer or shoemaker; he was followed by a girdler, a baker, two skinners, another baker, another skinner, another girdler, a butcher, a tailor, and so on. Other occupations named in the register for 1272–3 are mercer, leatherdresser, goldsmith, saddler, miller, tanner, and in the next year there was a mariner, several parchment-makers, a locksmith, a nailmaker, and two lorimers or harness-makers. As time goes on additional trades make their first appearance: a carpenter in 1275, a goldbeater in 1277, a bellfounder in 1283, a mason in 1294; in 1296 a plumber and a needle-maker, in 1299 a sawyer, in 1300 a wiredrawer. The first plasterer was made free in 1333, the first gardener in the following year, in 1343 the first bookbinder, Adam de Oxenforth, who settled in Stonegate, employed two servants, and lived on until 1390. The fact that he had his home in St Helen's parish means that it was in the lower half of the street, not in the Liberty of St Peter, where it would not have been essential for him to pay to take up the freedom of the city.

At times it seems that a whole new industry must have

been set up, for example that of coverlet-weaver, first mentioned in 1380 when eleven men of that trade became free of York. Only two of the eleven can be identified in the Poll Tax of the next year, 1381, John de Acastre in the parish of St Crux and William de Ellerker in St Sampson, both described as 'tapiter' or tapestry-maker. On the other hand, 18 tapiters had been admitted under that designation between 1366 and 1379, of whom only five, or possibly six, can be found still in the Poll Tax in 1381. Two points arise: the first is that caution must be exercised in assuming that two tradenames are necessarily two different crafts (carpenter and wright are another instance of identity). Secondly, it seems certain that the taxation records must be far from complete, to an extent that goes beyond what can be accounted for by damage and illegibility.

It is from the Poll Tax of 1381, at any rate relatively complete for the whole city, that we can get some idea of the main trades practised and also of the parts of the city where the men of each craft congregated. Setting aside the victuallers and the merchants, the numerous groups were the 75 weavers (as well as 13 tapiters), the 73 tailors, the 32 drapers; the 44 tanners and 44 cordwainers, the 23 saddlers and 20 skinners; the 36 wrights and carpenters and 16 tilers; the 22 smiths of various types, the 11 goldsmiths and 11 founders and potters. Most of these would have been numerous in any mediaeval city, and it is some of the smaller bodies that were particularly distinctive of York. Such were the six glaziers and 13 masons, the two bookbinders and three scriveners, the three gardeners, five horners, six painters, and the single clockmaker, a pioneer. There were five shipwrights, all in the parishes of St Clement and St Mary the Old (i.e. Bishophill Senior), showing that the maritime quarter of York was still the archbishop's fee to the south-west of the river in and near Clementhorpe.

York must already have had large numbers of visitors, for

there were 14 hostilers, eight cooks, and six taverners. We must understand 'cook' as meaning a restaurant proprietor. To serve the needs of the citizens there were also seven brewers and a vintner, and it seems likely that in some cases at least a brewer kept some sort of hostelry. Both cooks and brewers were in the well-to-do class that had property to leave and made wills; so too were saucemakers, of whom there were three in 1381 assessed to the tax. In several instances a man described in one context as a saucemaker appears elsewhere as a mustardmaker, so these terms were presumably alternatives for the same thing. The hostelries were well spread out, in twelve parishes of which only Holy Trinity (Christ Church) King's Court and St Denys, Walmgate, had two each. Some establishments were quite large, for in the surviving fragments of the tax for 1377, Thomas de Malton, cook, in the parish of St Martin, Coney Street, who had obtained the freedom in 1335, paid tax in respect of his wife and 13 servants. By 1381 he was dead, but his widow Cecilia was put down as a brewer and had with her a sister Margaret and three female servants. In 1459 an order was made that no aliens from foreign parts should lodge anywhere within the city or suburbs except at the Bull in Coney Street. This had probably only recently been built, or licensed as an inn; in the reign of Henry VII its name was changed to the Rose, but early in the sixteenth century it was in a ruinous state and mentions of the property cease after 1644. It was not, as Davies suggested but Angelo Raine disproved, identical with the George, and its position is not known. The George, of which we have seen the last remaining fragment, existed before 1455 and was demolished in 1869.

In the course of our wanderings we have seen a great deal of what survives structurally from the mediaeval city, even though it may have been rebuilt or restored in replica at least once or even repeatedly. Yet the York we see is recognisably the same city of 500 years ago. The profile of the Minster with its three towers, the Walls, many of the parish churches, the Guildhall, the Hall of the Merchant Adventurers, St Anthony's Hall, Clifford's Tower, St William's College, substantial remains of St Mary's Abbey and of St Leonard's Hospital, the plan of the main streets – all would be recognised by a mediaeval citizen if he were to come back. Most of the houses would be strange to him and he would be even more astonished than some of us to see the disproportionate size and height of some recent buildings. Yet he, looking forward, and we with hindsight, can appreciate that there has been a continuous process of development. Old Mother Shipton, whose tombstone is said to have been at Clifton, just outside the city, made as her most famous prophecy: 'Winchester was, London is, and York shall be, the fairest city of the three.' But she lived, if at all, in the reign of Henry viii, and it may be that York has now passed its hour . . .

Something has already been said of early development outside the Roman area and the changed crossing of the Ouse at the site of the old bridge. So much had happened before the Norman Conquest. The founding of religious houses, mostly soon after the Conquest, immobilised certain parts of the city for more than 400 years, and this process went even further when the friars had been settled in the thirteenth century. What was happening to York between the time of Henry i and that of Henry viii? It is safe to assume that there was a tendency to build up the area within the defences and that the wide open spaces were covered with middle rows and blocks of houses. We can see this happening in the case of Ousegate: late in the twelfth century it was called 'the great place named Ousegate', the word *placea*, as with the Spanish *plaza*, implying not only an open space but also a market. At that time there were presumably no buildings between High Ousegate and Coppergate, but by 1319 there is mention of a plot with a house on it stretch-ing from Ousegate in front to Coppergate behind.

Much later there were open agricultural fields at points within the city boundaries, notably in the Hungate district where two 'selions' or strips of land were granted in the parish of St John in 1427. Land in the fields of York and Bootham was still in open strips long after the end of the Middle Ages, and we have to remember that until the nineteenth century the interests of town and country were closely intermingled. Cowkeeping remained until recent times a major occupation of the suburbs, putting herds of cows out upon the Strays by day, but having to bring them in at night to enclosed land not subject to rights of common. The driving of cattle to market inside the city was naturally one of the main reasons why money had to be spent upon paving. It was the arrival of Edward I and the courts in 1298, when York became a G.H.Q. for the Scottish war, that speeded improvements. The king required paving to be repaired, and the city was granted pavage, the right to raise a special rate for paving, in 1319 for ten years and in 1329 for another five years. The abbot of St Mary's in 1335 had a grant of pavage for four years for his borough of Bootham. It might seem that this activity would have completed the paving of the streets as a whole, but in 1387 a paviour, Robert Bakewell, was admitted to the freedom in considera-tion of his having made the pavement of Monkgate by contract. In 1424 it was the condition of a lease that the tenant of certain land was to maintain and repair the paving of the whole street of Gillygate.

The streets had not merely to be paved, but to be kept clean, and in 1485 there was an ordinance that the streets in both city and suburbs should be swept once every week. In 1550 all the inhabitants were ordered to sweep the streets before their dwellings twice a week, but the modern system arrived in 1580, when four scavengers were appointed to sweep all the streets every Tuesday, Thursday, and Saturday, one man to each ward, and to be paid by assessment. The streets had their names from a very early date, most of them being of Scandinavian origin, but they did not bear nameplates until 1782. Street lighting, on the other hand, was attempted before the end of the mediaeval period, but without much success. By 1472 it had been ordered that a lantern with a lit candle was to be hung at the gates of the Bedern every night, but this had not been done. In 1527 every city alderman of the select council known as the 24 was to have a lit lantern over his gate from 5 to 9 p.m., and in 1569 another order provided for lanterns to be set forth on moonless nights. In November 1580 every three or four householders were to collaborate in hanging out a lantern, but next year the rule was that lanterns should be hung before men's doors.

Superficially it might seem that progress was more or less regular, but there had been troughs of decline and impoverishment. Epidemics, especially the Black Death, caused temporary depopulation, and York shared to the full in the national economic decline of the fifteenth century. Piracy round the coasts became widespread, and in 1430 it was complained that many of the mercery of the city – the wealthy trading class – were reduced by misfortune at sea and were living on charity. The main sources of civic revenue were producing 40 per cent less in 1499 than they had in 1442. By 1487 the mayor wrote to Henry VII that the population was halved and the city so decayed as to be incapable of defence. All the same, we know that great works were carried out, not only the completion of the Minster, but the rebuilding of many parish churches, the Guildhall, and much else. In 1406 Foss Bridge was in ruins, and in the next few years pontage was granted and raised both for rebuilding it and for repairing Ouse Bridge which was weak and broken.

Taking a bird's-eye-view backwards over the Middle

Ages in York, we can see that the peak of achievement lay in the fourteenth century, in spite of the Black Death, the Hundred Years War, and political and economic turmoil. It was during the hundred years from 1300 to 1400 that great investment took place in property, building rents for the church and chantry estates. The licences which had to be obtained from the Crown to convey land into the perpetual 'dead hand' of a chantry give valuable information on just when strips of land – some of them on the edges of church-yards, as Holy Trinity Goodramgate in 1316 and St Peter-le-Willows Walmgate in 1396 – were built upon. In another case it is a building contract in a register of the Minster chapter that tells us of the building of a terrace of seven timber-framed houses in 1335 by the north side of St Martin in Coney Street. Not only houses but trade was advancing: in 1366 the quay called the King's Staith below the bridge had just been built, and there were repeated grants of quayage for its maintenance until the end of the century. This too was the time when much of the best architecture was erected in the churches, and the finest glass painted.

After 1400 the waning of the Middle Ages had indeed set in, and this can most poignantly be felt in the increased insistence, in endowments and wills, on the need for soul Masses. It was not simply a movement of the rich to provide for their own spiritual well-being. The common man in the street, who could not afford to endow perpetual masses for himself, joined one of the religious fraternities formed for the purpose. They were mutual assurance societies, but directed to welfare after death rather than to a pensioned retirement. In York the great fraternity was the guild of Corpus Christi founded in 1408. It had seven main rules: that on the day of Corpus Christi the chaplains and two of the masters were to go in procession; that six chaplains be chosen yearly to rule the guild; the six masters to admit candidates who promised to contribute according to their means; the chaplains in their daily Masses to remember the brethren, living or dead; the lay members to say yearly for the souls of their departed brethren the Psalter of the Virgin; all brothers and sisters of the guild to attend Mass on Sunday within the octave of the feast and to give 2d each, and on that day there should be a sung Obit for the deceased members; on Corpus Christi day ten lights to be carried before the sacrament, and at a member's funeral six lights, the members paying 2d each a year to maintain these lights. The register of the guild still exists and has been printed. It contains the complete list of members admitted from the start until 1546, the last year before the abolition of such fraternities as superstitious; and a list of the Obits, or deaths of members year by year, from 1408 to 1437.

In reading the guild register one is struck by the catholicity of the membership, clerical and lay, rich and poor. In their religion as in their worldly lives, the men and women of York were thoroughly shaken together and well mixed. Large houses and small line the streets; nobleman, alderman, trader, craftsman, labourer rubbed shoulders together in the street and at the Mass; they likewise joined the guild and paid their dues, as well as leaving whatever legacy they could afford. York was far from being a democracy – for most of its mediaeval history it was a strict oligarchy – but in its beliefs it was united, a classless society. It was this fundamental unity of the people of York, indeed of Northerners as a body, that generated the deep feeling expressed in the Pilgrimage of Grace of 1536–7. Triggered by the suppression of the smaller monasteries, this was not just an outburst of religious conviction. Though defeated and its ringleaders executed – for rebellion against constituted law and order must be put down unless chaos is to ensue – the Pilgrimage secured its most important demand. No man whose dwelling was north of Trent should be required to appear at any King's Court except at York; and this was secured from 1537 by the reconstitution of the old King's Council in the North Parts. For 105 years York was the seat of the Lord President of the Council and the usual place of the Council sessions, an effective regional autonomy which, thanks to the wry methods of the Genius Loci, saved much from the wreck of the Middle Ages.

7 York Reformed

The chief lesson of history is that life goes on: maybe not that of particular individuals, but that of societies. Unless there is a massacre or a forced exodus, people have to carry on under changed conditions. This was eminently the case in York after the end of the Middle Ages. We have seen that in the middle of the reign of Henry VIII the city was strongly traditional, a centre of reaction against innovations in religion and social life; but on the other hand that, 200 years later when glaziers scribbled anti-Papist slogans on church glass, there was an opposite conservatism, loyal to the Elizabethan settlement of the Church as modified by Civil War, Restoration, and the Revolution of 1688. All the same, matters in York were seldom carried beyond verbal scrapping, and the Bar Convent and other Catholic institutions and personalities were generally respected. Fundamentally, York at both extremes remained a centre of moderation. It is true that it had its quota of appalling crimes: the martyrdoms of Valentine Freez and his wife as Protestants and of Margaret Clitherow for harbouring a Catholic priest stand as perpetual reminders of brutality equally vile on both sides. Yet somehow most people could adapt themselves.

Adaptation takes time, and it was a long time after the

25 Top left *John Carr's Castlegate House of 1759–63;* 26 right *No. 47, Bootham, one of Carr's earlier works,* c. 1753.

27 Left *Micklegate House, built in 1752 and attributed to Carr.*

28 Top left *A rainwater head on No. 71, Micklegate. The crest of the occupant of* c. *1745–50 dates the new brick front;* 29 right *A wrought-iron lamp-bracket at No. 54 Micklegate.*
30 Above left *Georgian doorhead in Bootham;* 31 right *The fifteenth-century carved brackets of the porch at 'Jacob's Well' in Trinity Lane.*

Pilgrimage of Grace and the dissolution of the monasteries before positive Protestantism became other than the exception in the North generally, as well as in York. It has been pointed out that more than a generation afterwards, in 1570, nearly two-thirds of the gentry of Yorkshire were still Catholic, 12 years after Elizabeth's accession. In a recent study of the transition Dr David Palliser has analysed in detail the evidence provided by the formulae used in wills of the twenty years 1534–53. Taking the known York wills from all sources, 312 altogether, he finds that in the years 1538–46 almost 96 per cent employed traditional Catholic forms, and none was specifically Protestant; in 1547–53, the reign of Edward vi, over 64 per cent were still traditional and only 8 per cent or less Protestant in any positive way. On the other hand, wills made before the monastic houses were dissolved show little attachment to other than parochial religion: out of 536 wills less than one-third made bequests to the York friaries and only a little over 12 per cent to any other religious house. Devotion was overwhelmingly to the 40 parish churches and in second place, a very long way behind, to the four orders of friars.

These hard facts make it much easier to understand Henry viii's assessment of the national situation. If even the traditionalist North cared so little for the maintenance of the monastic system, general public opinion would not be outraged at the abolition of the orders. Far too much of the national wealth in land and house property belonged to a limited category of slight devotion and by that time of increasingly slack and lazy life. It is striking that the one exception, apart from that of the friars, to the general indifference to the regulars consisted of bequests to local Charterhouses. It was recognised by many people that the Carthusian order did maintain genuine devotion and had not become corrupt. It is one of the most tragic aspects of the English Reformation – which indeed started with a desire for reform of much that needed amendment – that the king was not able to exercise discrimination in favour of the Carthusians, whose sincere devotion made them oppose his authority.

In York, as elsewhere, a whole crowd of opportunists was waiting in the wings to pick up a profit. The great market in ex-monastic property in the city found ready buyers, who seem to have had no difficulty in making a pretty penny within the next generation or so. Much detailed work remains to be done in analysis of the value of property as a source of income in York, as set against the steep inflation of the sixteenth century. It is well known that both monastic and chantry estates had a very poor yield in the last half-century of the old regime. Rents which had been adequate for the payment of mass-priests were no longer sufficient; maintenance of the rented houses was not kept up and these decayed, with further lowering of values. As we know from much more recent experience, a vicious circle is produced, commonly ending in demolition and redevelopment at great profit to third parties.

Long before the dissolution and the first breath of Protestantism in York, the founding of chantries had been brought to a premature close by the general poverty of the city. No new chantry was founded after 1510; no addition made to an existing chantry after 1529; more than half of the eighty parish chantries were in 1535 valued at figures below the legal minimum stipend of five marks (£3 6s 8d). A year later the corporation, which held the gift of a number of the chantries, obtained the dissolution of seven of them. Considering that it had been the clear intention of testators, in placing their property in the hands of the city authority, that it should be safeguarded in perpetuity, this operation was a flagrant though legalised breach of trust. This is brought home in startling fashion by the will of John Hag, a merchant free of the city in 1471 and a chamberlain in

1477, who died in 1499. He lived in Holgate Lane just off Blossom Street and held property there which was not to be sold but its profit devoted to prayers for the souls of Master Robert Bellamy, John Bellamy, and John Hag and Agnes his wife, 'giffyng them every yer a derige and a messe (Dirge and Mass) of Requiem sending the Belman furth aboute the Cite to make knowlege of the same – And this to be don of the morn after the Assumpcion of our lady while the world goth abowte'. The corporation was able to get its hands on the land in Holgate Lane, which continued to be called Hagg Closes until the middle of the nineteenth century when it was partly taken for the railway and the rest profitably built over with new streets.

That the period of the Dissolution and Reformation opened the way to a class of new rich gentry is a commonplace. At York these events of the sixteenth century seem to have enabled the local authority – the corporation – to recover the position of dominance which, through sheer lack of funds, it had been in danger of losing. It is easy, however, to sneer at the jumped-up Protestant capitalists and the smug aldermen, and there is another side to the medal. Like it or not, the destruction of the whole of the monasteries and chantries and almost all the colleges, the weakening of even secular cathedral establishments like York meant an enormous loss of patronage and thus of employment. An immense vacuum was left, speedily filled by the new nobility and gentry and by the municipalities. Hospitals, both for the sick and for the aged, and schools, formerly very generally in religious hands, were now founded or maintained by the new owners of property. The money had to come from somewhere, and it came out of profits. Whether the new inducements to such expenditure were better, because less superstitious, than the old is a point into which we need not inquire. England, and York, continued to be charitable and to pay tribute to learning. At the same time there may have been an increase in the cost-analysis view of life, just as there was an effective improvement in methods of book-keeping.

It was owing to the poverty of many church livings that an Act was obtained in 1547 providing for the union of benefices at the joint discretion of the archbishop and the city corporation. In all nineteen churches – half of the total in York – were threatened, but as we have seen, St Cuthbert, St Helen Stonegate, and St Martin Micklegate were saved by resolute action of individuals or bodies of parishioners, and this may also have resulted in the failure to proceed in the case of All Saints North Street. Thirteen churches were actually suppressed between 1547 and 1587, though the fabric of one, St Andrew, has survived. Two, St George and St Maurice, were not destroyed in the sixteenth century, but one became a ruin during the siege of 1644 if not earlier, and St Maurice was rebuilt on a new plan in 1876. The available evidence indicates that St Andrew's was typical of the very small churches suppressed, so that the architectural loss to the city was not so great as might be supposed, and certainly of less moment than the destruction in the last hundred years of old St Maurice, St Crux, and St Mary Bishophill Senior.

It was nevertheless true that the face of York was seriously changed for the worse in the middle of the sixteenth century. The loss of the monasteries, the friaries, and a dozen parish churches, even though small, was a grave aesthetic blow, equalled culturally by the almost total loss of the monastic libraries. Only the wholesale devastation of the historic scene in our own time can be compared to what befell in an equivalent period of the 1500s. We may ask whether York in exchange was compensated in any way. It has to be admitted that the corporation succeeded, by its somewhat ruthless policy, in restoring the economy. Its campaign, already mentioned, to uphold the dignity of the city by insisting that empty frontages be built up was a sound move and met with a degree of success. There are, or were until recently, large houses of the later sixteenth century that show exactly what replaced the slummy rents of later mediaeval times. They display the peak of development of the timber-framed building, of three main storeys with jetties, roofed with plain tiles on steep pitched roofs, sometimes containing an additional attic storey. It was with buildings of this type that much of the mediaeval two-storied town had been replaced before the onset of the Georgian period.

Monumental building had ceased at the Minster and, with the completion of St Michael-le-Belfrey in 1537, on the parish churches. The magnificent new arch of Ouse Bridge of 1565–6 was a really notable addition to the York scene, and so were the ranges added to the old Abbot's Lodging of St Mary's, now the King's Manor, by successive Lords President of the Council in the North. The earliest phase of work was that for Henry VIII in 1540–2, succeeded by that of Rutland, *c.* 1561–3, Radclyffe in 1568–70, Huntingdon in 1572–5, Sheffield in 1611–24, and lastly Strafford in 1634–6. The building was transformed into one of the outstanding palaces of its time, but was rivalled by the enlarged Archbishop's Palace leased to Sir Arthur Ingram, in which Charles I kept his court when in York. A third palace was built (from 1638) on Bishophill in a splendid position, by Thomas Lord Fairfax, and this later came by marriage to the second Duke of Buckingham and so was generally called Duke's Hall. The typical material was by this time brick, and bricklayers became more common as freemen of York after 1590. By 1645, as we have seen (above, p. 89) it was ordered that houses in the city should be built 'upright from the ground in brick', that is, that they were not only not to be of timber framing, but were not to have jettied overhangs. When King James VI of Scotland inherited the throne of England at Elizabeth's death in 1603, he visited York on his progress southwards, and the Bars were washed and painted, while the inhabitants were to paint their houses in colours ordered by the wardens.

What is certain is that the long depression that had begun far back in the fifteenth century gradually lifted from York after the middle of the sixteenth. There was a return of wealth, doubtless in part due to the permanent sessions of the Council and, after 1561, of the Ecclesiastical Commission for the northern province. The population began to rise and, apart from the immediate effects of the siege of 1644, there is no reason to think that it has ever again dropped. The rate of increase was, however, extremely slow until after 1760, when the total cannot have been very much greater than the 12,000 or so that is the likely figure for the city and inner suburbs about 1630. From 1632 until 1676 the city authorities carried out the assessment to the poor rate through all the parishes of the city as well as those of the Ainsty or county of the City of York, and in the 'Marches' of the city. This last category of parishes is of outstanding interest, since it must correspond approximately to the area 'round about' York, in so far as it was not included in city parishes. The places named were St Marygate, Clifton, Heworth, Heslington St Lawrence, Heslington St Paul, Osbaldwick, Gate Fulford, and Water Fulford. Naburn belonged to St George's in the city, Copmanthorpe and Upper Poppleton as well as Holgate to St Mary Bishophill Junior, Knapton and Dringhouses to Holy Trinity Micklegate, Middlethorpe to St Mary Bishophill Senior. Had they not been in the Ainsty, the parishes of Nether Poppleton, Acomb, Askham Bryan, Bishopthorpe, and Acaster Malbis would doubtless also have been reckoned in the marches of the city.

The information given as to relative wealth in different parts of York has already been mentioned, but these assessments are interesting in other ways. The total number of households accounted for, as either rated or pauper, was 840 in the city parishes in 1632, 859 in 1641, 895 in 1651, 1,070 in 1661, 1,125 in 1671, and 1,425 in 1676. Undoubtedly the earlier returns did not include by any means every house, since independent sources give the number of houses within the walls in 1639 as 1,786 and in the whole of the city parishes as 2,156. What is highly significant of the destruction caused by the siege is that comparison of the figures for 1644 and 1645 shows a loss of 21 rated households in the three suburbs outside Bootham Bar (11), Monk Bar (8), and Walmgate Bar (2), but in value these were about 1/25 of the whole assessment. The total drop in rated households was from 540 in 1632 to 488 in 1645, or roughly 10 per cent; evidently a number of the well-to-do inhabitants had left the city before the siege.

About this time the first detailed descriptions of York begin. John Leland had visited the city *c.* 1539, just after the dissolution, but what is left of his account (for a substantial part is certainly lost) gives very little information except about the walls. The earliest serious history was that of Sir Thomas Widdrington, recorder and then MP for York, finished about 1660 though not published until 1897. Roger Dodsworth, Sir William Dugdale, Matthew Hutton and, above all, James Torre, took copious notes from documents, church monuments, and glass windows, and Torre made plans and sketches of the Minster, but the first written perambulation of the city that has survived seems to be that made in 1680 by Henry Keepe (1652–88), who published a book on Westminster and hoped to do the same for the northern capital. Keepe, as an outsider and a southerner, was able to give an objective and remarkably unbiassed view of the place, from which it is worth quoting a few extracts.

'The Inhabitants of this city are verry civill and courteous, obliging to strangers who come out of curiosity as well as to forraigners for their trafick and commerce. . . . I take it to be one of the cheapest citys in Europe. . . . In the third

(Water Lane) called farr Waterlaine at my being there was a place erected where the sect called Quakers had their weekely meetings & assemblys. . . . Viccar lane where in stood heretofore the Colledg of S. William which is now a private house & belongs to Mr. Jenkins. Beyond this is that noted & most memorable place The Beddern where the Emperour Constantine the Great was borne. . . . And now by a stone Bridg of five Arches wee pass to the west side of the River Owse, Att the foot where of stands the Burse or Exchange, The Counsell-chamber, The Exchequer, The Sheriffs court, with the common prysons for the city, . . . ascending from hence up the hill that rises by degrees you come to one of the fairest, largest, longest & most comely streets of all the city called Micklegate or the great Street (all though Conney street be preferred before it . . .) att the end whereof is a port of Barr of the same name & Magnificence through which is the direct road to London. . . . In this gracefull street are three parish churches to advance its beauty, viz. S. John's, S. Martyn's, And that of the Holy Trinity. . . . For the suburbs on this side they are not very larg containeing onely one street without Micklegate-barr, where in stands the two Hospitalls of S. Katherine & S. Thomas . . . Leaving this suburb wee cross the water againe not by the Bridg but by boate or the ferry which brings us to the suburb on east-side Owse where by Bootham wee behold the ruins of the famious Abby of S. Mary, now called the Mannour where the Governours (or deputies for ye King) usually reside. . . . And thus I have given you the . . . progress or perambulation through . . . places of note or name in this city according as they where (*sic*) shown and related to mee by Mr. Andrew Davye an antient native here, a great lover of this his birthplace and not a little verst in Antiquities . . .'

Strictly antiquarian interest in York had begun a century earlier at least, for William Camden had noted finds of 1579 when collecting material for his *Britannia*. There is therefore a tradition of four centuries behind the acceptance of the city as something highly exceptional and worthy of study because of its age and renown, and for its famous and beautiful streets and buildings. This is important, as disproving the suggestion often made, that the attitude of mind underlying conservation is a modern growth and a stultifying negation of progress. The work of Camden was continued by Dodsworth and the rest, and the deliberate collection of material from the Minster and churches by Dugdale in 1641 was a crash-programme undertaken in the light of probable destruction by the impending hostilities of the Civil War. The protection given to both the monuments and the libraries and records of York by the two Fairfaxes, father and son (Ferdinando the second and Thomas the third baron Fairfax of Cameron) showed that concern for the preservation, both of the physical city and its culture, had become a prominent factor at the highest level, even in the midst of warfare.

Another aspect of this interest in historic York was shown by the artists who began at that time to record its beauties in drawings, paintings, and engravings. The first general views to survive are amateurish drawings by Gregory King, Dugdale's assistant on the heraldic visitation of 1665–6 when a boy of 17. Similar but far better views were drawn some ten to twelve years later by the two friends Francis Place and William Lodge, and Place produced many detailed drawings of York buildings over a period of some fifty years. Survey plans too were made, beginning with the small but accurate work of John Speed in 1610, and in the next two hundred years including six or seven independent surveys of the built-up area before the Ordnance Survey produced the first precise and detailed plans in 1846–53.

It is a problem whether this marked and increasing interest in York's historic past and in the surviving antiquities was in some sense a psychological compensation for a sinking material position. No really satisfactory explanation of the extreme and protracted depression suffered by York has ever been given. It was certainly connected with the decline of the textile industry, but it is not at all clear why this should have happened. We have seen that coverlet-weavers and tapiters became freemen in large numbers in the second half of the fourteenth century, and that this particular trade remained of importance is demonstrated by the 1542 Assize of Coverlets, an act which gave to the city a monopoly of this craft in Yorkshire. The preamble to the act refers to York as having been maintained 'most principally by making and weaving of coverlets and coverings for beds'; the inhabitants in great number in the city and suburbs had 'been daily set on work in spinning, dyeing, carding, and weaving of the said coverlets'. It has been said that York faced competition from the West Riding, but it is not clear why it was defeated. The suspicion remains that the decisive factor was the extreme position taken up by the corporation in closing the freedom by putting up the fees beyond the level that could be afforded by young men of enterprise who wished to set themselves up in the city. It may well have been self-defeating protectionism.

It cannot be claimed that York, during the sixteenth and seventeenth centuries, was the birthplace of very many famous men, though some were settlers in the city for longer or shorter periods. Guy Fawkes must be considered notorious rather than famous, but he was son of the registrar of the Consistory Court of York and had a good education at the Grammar School. Guy was baptised in the church of St Michael-le-Belfrey on 16 April 1570, but his birthplace has only very recently been firmly identified, by the researches of Miss K. M. Longley. It can now be said that the conspirator was born somewhere in the large house Nos. 32, 34 Stonegate, on the north-west side below the Star Inn and the property next to the boundary of St Helen's parish. The Fawkes home was, however, not merely in St Michael's but belonged to the dean and chapter. The birth of Sir Thomas Herbert near Pavement has been mentioned: he won distinction as a traveller in Persia, the East Indies, and Africa, and published a *Description of the Persian Monarchy* in 1634, five years after his return. As a Parliamentarian he was appointed to attend on Charles I in 1646 during the king's captivity, and became a devoted royalist, reaping the reward of a baronetcy at the Restoration.

Among residents in York were Dr Martin Lister, FRS, from 1670 to 1683, when he had several scientific books printed by John White of the Stonegate establishment opposite to the Star. Among these works was Lister's translation of Johannes Godartius *Of Insects*, with plates drawn and etched by Francis Place. Lister, a close friend of the great naturalist John Ray, was the first to suggest the preparation of geological and soil maps in 1683, and while he lived in York was on terms of particular friendship with the artistic circle centred round Place, who leased from the Crown a suite of apartments in the King's Manor, in the front range to north of the main entrance. Place's friend and fellow artist, William Lodge, was a Leeds man and related to Ralph Thoresby, and another member of the circle, Thomas Kirke of Cookridge near Leeds, was associated with the great Leeds historian. Another kind of science was practised in York at the same time by George Villiers, the second Duke of Buckingham, who added a laboratory to the great house on Bishophill, for experiments in chemistry and alchemy. But, wrote Drake, 'if he did not find out the philosopher's stone . . . it is certain he knew a way of dissolving, or evaporating, gold and other metals, quicker than any other man of that age'.

Another group or club of men with artistic and antiquarian interests, also linked with Thoresby, has been mentioned in connection with No. 68 Micklegate. Not only Henry Gyles the glass-painter, but his nephew Samuel Smith, a bell-founder and Sheriff of York in 1723–4, Samuel Carpenter, carver and statuary (1660–1713), and John Etty the painter, who died in 1707, belonged to this body of friends. Carpenter was the sculptor of the exquisite bust of Lady Elizabeth Stapleton (1683) at Snaith in the south of Yorkshire and worked at Castle Howard. Etty predeceased his father, the more famous John Etty (1633–1708), the carpenter and architect. The family, not related to that of the later painter William Etty, lived in North Street and the father, who was associated with Wren and Grinling Gibbons, had his epitaph in All Saints, telling us that he 'by the strength of his own genius and application had acquired great knowledge of Mathematicks especially Geometry and Architecture in all its parts, far beyond any of his Contemporaries in this City'. The tablet was probably put up some time after his death, as it mistakenly asserts that he died on 28 January 1709, aged 75; but the parish register shows that his burial really took place on 30 January 1707/8.

Apart from the King's Manor, not much architecture now visible survives from the period of the Reformation to Revolution. Some work actually done on surviving buildings, such as the tower of St Martin-cum-Gregory (1677), has been re-gothicised. The little timber-framed belfry of St John Micklegate is of 1646, and the additions to St Anthony's Hall are of the same date, as is the house we noted on the corner of Petergate and Stonegate. A sprinkling of the jettied and gabled houses in the older parts of York, reputedly mediaeval, are really of the late sixteenth and early seventeenth centuries. Even in the interiors of churches there are not very many fittings of the time, though the pulpit of St Martin in Micklegate is of 1636 and is like another at All Saints Pavement; in All Saints North Street is one of 1675. An unusual type of wooden font-cover, with inverted scrolls, is found in several churches, and has been documented by the Royal Commission on Historical Monuments within the period 1638–1717. There are some good memorial tablets in baroque style, but mostly after 1700, though the magnificent achievement of the Royal Arms in stained glass by one of the Gyles in Acomb church, just outside the city, is of 1663. No doubt many structural and decorative features remain throughout York, but they make little visual impact.

The period was then one of transition. As we now see it, it is to a surprising extent still mediaeval in appearance, and contributes to the overall impression of York as an antique city. In spite of the preponderance of brick Georgian fronts and houses, York has little likeness to Bath or the traditional streets and squares of London or Dublin. The older plan with its strangely cockeyed intersections and divergences from Roman alignments still rules and provides as it were a bony structure dominant through the skin-deep Georgian frontwork, or even new building on the old plots. This reluctance to make fundamental changes in the streetscape of the city was, even if subconsciously, the outcome of the admiration felt for York's historic quality. The antiquarian approach, from Camden, Dodsworth, and Dugdale on to Hutton, Torre, and Keepe, proved valid, and set up a living and fruitful tradition.

8 Modern York

We have seen that York, by the seventeenth century, had come to be culturally dominated by a tradition of its antiquity and beauty. This tradition has been handed down to our own day in spite of the enormous losses of much of the physical content which had been the origin of this idea of the city. Both depression and prosperity have taken their toll of York: depression by allowing the churches and houses to decay beyond repair; prosperity by providing the money for rebuilding and for that kind of development in which men speculate to accumulate. The great period of depression lasted from about 1400 until the reign of Elizabeth 1, when there was a partial recovery. The fact that in 1680, as reported by Keepe, it was one of the cheapest cities of Europe undoubtedly means that there was then another wave of at least relative depression; and in the early nineteenth century there was a further economic recession from which York was saved by George Hudson's manipulation of the railway net. York still is in our own day notoriously a place of low wage rates, even though it cannot now be described as cheap.

It is a striking fact that adversity, rather than prosperity, leads to real as opposed to fallacious progress. The lonely

stand of the United Netherlands in the sixteenth and seventeenth centuries, the regeneration of Denmark after the
disastrous defeat of 1864, the resurgence of Germany after
reaching the depths in 1945, are well-known examples of
this function. The growth of the British Empire can be
traced back, more than to any other single factor, to the
final loss of Bordeaux in 1453: out of despair arose a new
hope and a fresh achievement. The converse is now self-
evident: never in the whole of recorded history has mankind
appeared so bankrupt as in the recent age of growth and the
so-called affluent society.

The application of these general principles to the special
case of the city of York is of outstanding interest. Economic
depression hung over it like an almost perpetual thunder-
cloud after it had lost, about 1398, its last chance of becoming a major capital, even the chief city of England in
substitution for London. The downfall of Richard II, the
visionary sovereign who had dreamed of escape from the
purse strings of the Lombard Street of his time, for ever
crushed the aspirations of the northern metropolis. Even the
concept of York as the eponymous home of what, by magical
coincidence, became the Yorkist and legitimate cause, was
cruelly overthrown when the severed head of Richard duke
of York, crowned in paper, was set over Micklegate Bar
at midwinter. The ensuing spring, the March of 1461, saw
the triumph of the earl of March, Richard's son, as Edward
IV, but the gay garden planted by the 'fair rose and herb'
was not set in York.

Necessity is the mother of invention, and it is to York's
necessity that we owe a great deal in what may broadly be
termed the field of applied science. This will become clear
as we study the leading personalities of the city in the
modern age – the three centuries that have gone by since the
Revolution of 1688. There is, of course, nothing sacrosanct
about the Revolution in itself. It happens to mark a division

more clearly than any other event within the great trans-
formation of England that started at the Restoration of 1660
and the effective transfer of responsibility to Walpole as
prime minister between 1721 and 1730. Certainly it was
within that overall period that York acquired most of the
attributes that belong to the modern world. An effective
piped water supply was installed between 1677 and 1685,
official street lighting was brought in, a public bath-house
opened in 1691, the General Post Office established, and a
regular service of stage coaches to London started in 1703.
The amenities were improved by planting trees in Lord
Mayor's Walk in 1718 and on the Baile Hill in 1722 and
1726, and by forming the New Walk in 1731. The earliest
newspaper, the *York Mercury*, began in 1719, to be followed
in 1725 by the more famous and successful *York Courant*.
The Mansion House and the Assembly Rooms were built,
and in 1727 an act was passed for improving the navigation
of the Ouse. The Friars' Gardens, taken over in 1695 by
George Telford, were becoming under his son John the most
important nursery in the North and, as Drake put it, bringing 'our northern gentry into the method of planting and
raising all kinds of forest trees, for use and ornament'.

What particularly distinguished York was the practice of
medicine. It was the home of a long series of physicians, surgeons, and apothecaries of distinction. In 1740–3 it obtained
the first general hospital north of Trent, thanks to the
bequest of Lady Elizabeth Hastings (1682–1739), and so
became the main teaching school, in medicine and anatomy,
outside London. Whereas London had been fortunate in
saving both its great hospitals for the sick, St Bartholomew's
and St Thomas's, at the dissolution, York had altogether lost
its magnificent double foundation of St Peter's and St
Leonard's in December 1539. York made up for lost time
in the eighteenth century, but had already had the benefit of
several outstanding medical men. Among the first of these

32 Top *The Bar Convent, with Thomas Atkinson's main front of 1786–9, and the handsome houses of Blossom Street.*

33 Above *The majestic curve of York Railway Station, the largest in the world when it was opened in 1877.*

34   Top left *John Carr* (*1723–1807*), *architect;* 35 right *William Peckitt* (*1731–95*), *reviver of glass-painting.*
36   Above left *Tate Wilkinson* (*1739–1803*), *actor manager;* 37 right *James Atkinson* (*1759–1839*), *surgeon and bibliophile.*

was Dr Robert Wittie (1613–84), who practised here for twenty years before moving to London, publishing there in 1660 a book on *Scarborough Spaw*. Martin Lister, already mentioned as a scientist, became physician to Queen Anne. Clifton Wintringham (1689–1748), who built what is now the Judge's Lodgings, exercised his profession in York for 35 years and was the first physician to the County Hospital. Wintringham's successor as occupier of the house in Lendal, Dr John Dealtry, 'whose skill in his profession was only equalled by the humanity of his practice', died while visiting his patients in 1773 at the age of 65.

The first honorary surgeon to the County Hospital was Francis Drake the historian of York, City Surgeon from 1726. He was deprived in 1745 for refusing to take the oath of fealty to the Government at the time of the '45 rebellion. Like his colleague Dr John Burton, the gynaecologist and author of *Monasticon Eboracense*, Drake was a strong Tory with Jacobite sympathies. The two antiquaries, at that crucial time, set out together to survey 'some Roman Curiosities, found in a Field near Millington, on the Wolds'. As Drake recorded, 'whilst we were upon the Spot & directing this Survey, in the Year 1745, a Year in which the House of Stewart again attempted to recover the British Crown, some People observing us, gave an Information at York, that we were marking out a Camp in the Wolds; which had like to have occasioned us some Trouble to contradict'. Burton was actually imprisoned in the Tower of London for a time and there met Flora Macdonald. Burton followed up his acquaintance and obtained from her first-hand details which he published in 1749 as *A genuine and true Journal of the most miraculous escape of the Young Chevalier*. In 1751 he brought out in two volumes *An Essay towards a complete new System of Midwifery*, a pioneer work with copperplates drawn and etched by the young George Stubbs.

Stubbs, born in Liverpool in 1724, was a self-taught

painter and at the age of 20 had set up at Leeds as a portrait-ist. He must have realised that his knowledge of anatomy was inadequate and moved to York to take advantage of the newly opened hospital. He learned anatomy from dissection, then uncommon, and from Charles Atkinson, another of the York surgeons, so well that Stubbs soon got employment as a lecturer to York medical students. He spent nine or ten years in York and it was there that he first conceived the idea of the studies in comparative anatomy, beginning with the horse, that proved him one of the great naturalists as well as a supreme painter. But in his plates for Dr Burton's treatise, immature as they were, there is already manifest his deep and passionate search for complete truth in representation. Burton and his book were attacked, by the ruling clique of Whigs and purely from political odium. Sterne's cruel caricature of 'Dr Slop' reflects as much discredit upon its author as credit is due to the victim, whose ungainly body hid a noble heart. In an age of little charity Burton rode long rounds to visit the sick poor and justified himself by saying: 'I will at any time very willingly do my best to save any person, especially the poor and helpless: to do this I think is my duty and everyone's whom God hath enabled to do it.'

John Gowland, born in the parish of St Martin Coney Street in 1704, was apothecary to George I and George II and spent most of his life away from York; but two other apothecaries, father and son, spent most of their lives here. They were Theophilus Garencieres (1715–84) and Theophilus Davye Garencieres (1742–1803), who practised in Blake Street and was Lord Mayor in 1796. They were descended from the great French doctor, Theophilus Garencières (1610–80), who took his degree at Caen but on becoming a Protestant settled in England. Two more surgeons call for mention: James Atkinson (1759–1839), the son of Charles, a founder of the Yorkshire Philosophical Society and of the York Musical Society as well as a book collector on a grand scale; and Sir William Stephenson Clark, Lord Mayor in 1839, whose house in Micklegate we have seen. We also visited the home on Bishophill of Dr Stephen Beckwith the philanthropist; his grandiose tomb in Gothic style is in the Minster.

Before leaving the subject of medicine something should be said of The Retreat, the Quaker institution for the care of the mentally afflicted. The founder was William Tuke (1732–1822), a prominent grocer, who was one of the fourth generation from the first Tuke Friend who had joined George Fox in the middle of the seventeenth century. The unsatisfactory treatment of the insane moved Tuke to consider the possibility of founding something better, run by Friends for Friends, in 1790. Land was bought in 1793 on a splendid hilltop site towards Heslington, plans were obtained in 1794 from John Bevans, and the building was opened in 1796. The great superiority of the methods used at The Retreat was recognised from the start and in our own time L. A. G. Strong has written that 'a powerful, tranquillising spirit pervades these walks and walls and gardens'. The Retreat was by no means the only York institution due to the Tuke family, who also originated the girls' school now The Mount, in 1784, and in 1818 the idea of a boys' school which became Bootham School in 1829. Among the superintendents of The Retreat was Dr John Thurnam (1810–73) who was not only a leading authority on insanity but an outstanding anthropologist.

Medicine is the form of applied science which makes the most obvious impact on the average human life, but it was only one facet of the busy technological life of York. Some of the skilled crafts of the Middle Ages, already mentioned, represented the beginnings of York industries. The whole history of one of these crafts, that of the horners and combmakers, has been traced by Mr L. P. Wenham, from 1295 when it was already in being, down to 1931 when it came to an end with the firm of Rougier, established about 1794 and the source of the name Rougier Street, well known as that of the York bus station. The detailed story of the York clockmakers and watchmakers with a list of them from 1471 down to the mid-nineteenth century was told by T. P. Cooper. The Poll Tax of 1381, not in print in Cooper's time, carries the tale back for almost another century, to John Lovell, 'orlogemaker', who was living in the parish of St Mary Castlegate with his wife Agnes. Lovell had taken up the freedom in 1374, but as a goldsmith. The association between the crafts of goldsmith and silversmith and that of clockmaker has of course continued, in York as elsewhere. In York there was an assay office for silver from 1561 and important pieces of plate were made until soon after 1700, but the York mark has not been found between 1713 and 1778, and from that date onwards York silverware was of comparatively little importance. The city's most famous clockmaker, as we have seen, was Henry Hindley; the last of the famous silversmiths and watchmakers were the partners James Barber, Lord Mayor in 1833, and Robert Cattle, Lord Mayor in 1841, whose shop was in Coney Street.

Another York trade which was studied in depth, by George Benson, was that of the bell-founders. They formed one of the most notable of the technological crafts and were already flourishing at the start of the fourteenth century. The greatest of the family firms were those of Oldfield, which flourished from 1588 to 1650, when they were succeeded by the Smiths, already mentioned, in a foundry at Toft Green continuing to 1731; and the Sellers. The Seller foundry was at Jubbergate, in the centre of the city, and lasted from 1662 to 1764. The last York founder was George Dalton, in Stonegate and later in Lendal, from 1750 to 1791. Oddly enough, no sooner had bronze-founding died out than iron-foundries were set up in York, unlikely as this may seem. The most important was that of the Walker family, Victoria Foundry in Walmgate.

The making of various kinds of instruments seems to have been an offshoot of the several metal-working trades. At the end of the eighteenth century there were a number of plane-makers, among them Michael Varvill, who was at first in High Ousegate but later moved across the Bridge. It must be remembered that, apart from the simple joiner's plane, complex moulding planes were made which enabled panel-ling, picture-frames and other details to be produced economically. Plane-making thus played an important part in connection with building and cabinet-making and pre-ceded the modern machine-tool industry. The important York glass industry, making bottles, jars and many other commercial products, was founded in 1794 by John Prince (1749–1835) a jeweller, but son and grandson of York bricklayers and builders. A later development was the production of optical lenses and telescopes, microscopes and other instruments, by Thomas Cooke. He started his business in 1837 and by 1856 was able to build the large Buckingham Works on the site of the Duke of Buckingham's house on Bishophill; as Thomas Cooke & Sons Ltd the firm continued and eventually formed part of the amalgamation Cooke, Troughton & Simms, internationally famous.

Quite another side of applied science is represented in York by the wholesale trade in pharmaceutical drugs. This presumably took its rise as a result of the strongly medical interests of the city and was perhaps also connected with the concentration of gardens and nurseries in York from an early date, of which more will be said. One unique relic survives from the mediaeval compounding of drugs, the magnificent bronze mortar of the Infirmary of St Mary's Abbey, cast by Brother William de Touthorp in 1308. First reported in 1734, by Thomas Gent, the mortar was lost for many years but was eventually secured for the Yorkshire Museum. The drug trade of more recent times begins with George Ewbank, already a druggist in Castlegate by 1738, the year of birth of his son George. The son carried on the business after his father had retired to take up banking and the firm, after passing through several partnerships joined that founded in 1818 by John Raimes which, in 1897, had taken over Micklegate House. A third York business in the same field was started in Colliergate in 1780 by John Dales, Lord Mayor in 1816 and 1829; this was later Butterfield & Clarke and then Bleasdale Ltd. A glimpse of the background of the trade in earlier times is given by the obituary of Duke Holborne, a York gardener who died at the age of 77 in 1837. Holborne had been a Blue Coat boy, was then apprenticed for seven years to Robert Young, a well known York gardener, and took up the freedom in 1787. He held jobs as a gardener with various families, but 'for many years eked out a living by selling herbs to druggists'.

The gardens of York were of importance from an early date and after London formed the main centre of the nursery business. It is impossible to distinguish between the various types of gardening before about 1700 and many of the recorded gardeners probably kept market gardens for the supply of vegetables to the city. Starting in 1334, gardeners took up the freedom, and three were recorded in 1381, as well as fruiterers who in all probability grew the fruit they sold. As has been said, the Friars' Gardens on the site of the Dominican precinct – and very likely the garden of the ancient royal palace of before 1227 – were leased by George Telford from 1695 and had a continuous history until the railway took over the ground for the Old Station. This nursery was only the chief of several which flourished in the eighteenth century, significantly in the former precincts of other religious houses. The family of Bearpark had part of the site of St Mary's Abbey; a succession of gardeners had the Trinity Gardens off Micklegate; and Thomas Rigg took part of the land that had belonged to St Andrew's Priory in Fishergate. The Whartons, who had held the lease of the Friars' Gardens before the Telfords, moved to the Grey Friars below Castlegate. It was reported in the *York Courant* of 20 March 1760 that on the previous night Matthew Wharton's garden had been broken into by some person who 'cut down 463 Elms, from five to twelve feet high; 335 Cherry stocks; 4 Damsins; 19 standard Pears; and cut up part of a large Flat of Pease . . .' Rewards offered by Wharton and later, in the *London Gazette*, by the Town Clerk, do not seem to have produced any information on the criminal.

The interest in the purely ornamental side of gardening goes back a long way. There was a Florists' Feast held in 1740 at Gibson's in Lendal, and one in 1742 at Gainford's in Goodramgate, when a gold ring was the prize for the best carnation. The first of these was probably Henry Gibson, a somewhat shadowy figure who took several apprentices between 1733 and 1754; the other was Francis Gainford or Gainforth who took up the freedom in 1713 and in 1729 supplied trees for the Lord Mayor's garden and Common Hall Yard, behind the newly built Mansion House. He was a churchwarden of Holy Trinity in 1752 and still alive in 1758. It is not known whether there was any formal organisation of these early florists, but on 20 April 1768 there was founded what is now known as the Ancient Society of York Florists, a body which brought together amateurs and professionals and men from all classes of society. The first signature on the roll was that of the surgeon Charles Atkinson and other early members were John Telford junior, John Roebuck, William Adcock, Thomas Halfpenny, Joseph Perfect, and Andrew Thompson, nurserymen, and head gardeners; the botanist Robert Teesdale from Castle Howard; T. D. Garencieres the apothecary; the younger George Ewbank from Castlegate and James Wiggins of Pavement, another druggist. Detailed rules were drawn up

and frequent shows held for Hyacinths, Auriculas, Poly-
anthus, Tulips, Ranunculus, and Carnations in their seasons.

The interest in gardening, combined with the long tradition of printing in York, produced a small crop of books.
The first, by John Kennedy who was gardener to Sir Thomas
Gascoigne, Bart, was *A Treatise upon Planting, Gardening,
and the Management of the Hot-House*, published in 1776;
then William Speechly, gardener to the Duke of Portland,
brought out two standard works of the first class, *A Treatise
on the Culture of the Pine-Apple*, in 1779, and *A Treatise on the
Culture of the Vine*, in 1790. Next came the book of an
amateur dilettante, Richard Steele, *An Essay upon Gardening*,
of 1793. Evelyn's *Sylva* was reprinted in 1776 at York, with
notes by Dr Alexander Hunter who practised in York from
1763 and was the real founder of the York Lunatic Asylum
in Bootham Park, begun in 1772 and opened five years later.
Though the books were illustrated with engraved plates,
these are not of outstanding artistic or botanical interest. A
much later work, David Wooster's *Alpine Plants* of 1874,
with over one hundred coloured plates, obtained many of
the then rare plants from which they were drawn from the
York nursery of Backhouse & Son which had, for the last
thirty or forty years, pioneered in this line of introductions.

There was a surprising gap in the succession of York
artists during much of the eighteenth century. Francis Place
died in 1728 and was the last survivor of his age. In that
same year John Haynes became free as a saddler, but took
up engraving and land surveying. In 1740 he advertised that
he printed on leather for saddlers and surveyed land, and
also 'draws Perspective Views of Gentlemen's Seats'. Haynes
carried out archaeological surveys as well as estate plans, and
after moving to London about 1750 he published the
valuable engraved plan of the Chelsea Physic Garden and in
1755 made a large survey of Burghley Park for the Earl of
Exeter. The noted portrait painter Philip Mercier, born in

Berlin of Huguenot parents but settled in London, moved to York and lived here from 1739 to 1751 in the Minster Liberty. Apart from occasional visits by artists of national fame, such as that of Turner in 1797, York was singularly lacking in painters and draughtsmen for over a generation.

Thomas Beckwith, the herald painter, employed his friend Edward Abbot to make drawings of York buildings, as has been mentioned, but Abbot's work was very crude. Quite suddenly a group of York draughtsmen appeared within a short time: Joseph Halfpenny, Henry Cave, and John Browne. As we have seen, Halfpenny was a remarkable pioneer in the portrayal of mediaeval architecture, but it was rather Cave who was typical of the York tradition in that he came from a family steeped in the technique of whitesmith's work and was the son of an engraver, William Cave (1751–1812), who had been the apprentice of Robert Holme or Holmes, Ledger's brother-in-law and successor in Petergate. Henry Cave's etchings of *Picturesque Buildings in York*, issued in 1813, is the best single record of the old city. Like Browne, the historian and artist of the Minster, Cave earned his living largely as a drawing master.

The city's great tradition of glass-painting, from far back in the Middle Ages, has been touched upon, and its continuance through the seventeenth century in the persons of Edmund and Henry Gyles, to be finally revived by the idiosyncratic career of William Peckitt. During the eighteenth century York was also the home of a family of distinguished sculptors, the Fishers. Their pedigree is mysterious, since few of them left wills, and they moved from one address to another: furthermore, they were prolific, and repeatedly used the same Christian names. What is certain is that the first carver of the family, Richard Fisher, moved to York from Ripon in 1746 after executing works at Leeds, Ripon, and for country houses including Studley Royal where the chief gardener and clerk of works, William

Fisher (died 1743) was probably his father. Richard had married Alice Broadley at Ripon in 1730 and by her had several children, of whom John Fisher the elder (1735–1804) was likewise a noted statuary. At least ten of the family, over four generations, worked as sculptors in York, and in the last generation they also produced an architect, Charles Fisher (1829–92) who was the articled pupil of G. T. Andrews, and designed the new chancel of Holy Trinity, Micklegate, in 1886.

The architects of York in the eighteenth century and the early nineteenth are numerous and distinguished. In our perambulations we have come across the works of several of them. The most interesting practice, which still survives today, is the one handed down from John Carr 'of York' through a long succession of partnerships: with Peter Atkinson the elder, his son of the same name, the latter's sons J. B. and W. Atkinson, and so down. Carr's greatest contemporary in York was Thomas Atkinson (1729–98), no relation to Peter, the son and grandson of bricklayers and particularly remembered for his work of 1763–9 at Bishopthorpe Palace. He also built for himself a fine house in St Andrewgate, No. 20, now in sadly dilapidated condition. His best work in the city is the Bar Convent of 1765–75 with its main front of 1786–9. The later architects J. P. Pritchett and G. T. Andrews were both involved in the architecture of the early railway age, and were among the last outstanding exponents of Georgian classicism, along with J. B. and W. Atkinson.

John Carr, though not born in York, was a Yorkshireman and of such surpassing fame that his career deserves more than a passing mention. His origin is well known, thanks largely to the detailed researches of Robert Davies finished shortly before his death in 1875. Carr was born at Horbury near Wakefield in 1723, the son of Robert Carr a stonemason and quarry-owner, and was himself trained as a working mason. In early life he married Sarah Hinchcliffe of Felkirk, more than ten years older than himself and said to have been in domestic service at Bretton Hall where he was one of the masons. In his youth Carr was certainly poor, for he himself used to say: 'I have many a time had to lie in bed whilst my breeches were mending.' Within a few years, however, he was getting commissions. The first of these to bring him near to York came in 1749–50 when he built a new front and added a stable block to Askham Richard Hall, one of the country seats of the Garforth family, whose town house we have seen at No. 54 Micklegate. Carr was already living in the city of York by 4 October 1751 when he bought his first piece of property, a house 'with a Raff Yard, Garth, and a Kiln' in Skeldergate for £180. He described himself as 'mason', and was put down as 'stone-cutter' when he took up the freedom in 1756. This was just after he had built the Grandstand on the Knavesmire to his own designs, chosen in 1754 in preference to those of James Paine. When, in 1765, he bought a much larger Skeldergate property for £580 he was already calling himself an architect. Apart from his professional career Carr played a prominent role in civic affairs, as a chamberlain in 1766, sheriff the next year, alderman in 1769, and twice Lord Mayor, in 1770 and 1785. Many anecdotes are told of Carr's cheerful and powerful personality, and of his fine singing voice. In 1789 at York Races, attended by the Prince of Wales and the Duke of York, Carr was asked to entertain the royal visitors and 'delighted the company by singing, with admirable spirit and sweetness, the well-known patriotic ballad called "Hearts of Oak" '.

The architectural and building craftsmen of York between 1700 and 1850 were very numerous, but the most important of them formed veritable dynasties. Among the carpenters and joiners, some of whom also took up bricklaying and contracting, there were five generations of Etty, four of

Hansom culminating in Joseph Aloysius, six of Raisin or Rayson, from Richard Rason free in 1664 to his great-great-great-grandson Thomas Rayson (1792–1828). In another line of descent the original Richard's grandson Richard Raisin (1712–1801) was said at his death to have been '60 years a master builder in York'. The bricklayers could show three generations of Clough, as many of Fentiman, and four of Gray; and the stonemasons included three generations of Kilvington and two of Stead. Many of these men undoubtedly designed, with the help of copy-books, the houses they put up, and it is to them that a very high proportion of the sound construction and seemliness of the streets is due.

It is unnecessary to say much of the great tradition of York printers and booksellers, for Robert Davies devoted a whole book, *A Memoir of the York Press* (1868), to the authors, printers, and stationers from 1497 to 1789, and T. P. Cooper studied both 'The Sign of the Bible' in Stonegate and 'The Sign of the Crown' in Minster Gates, two of the greatest of York bookshops. York's first printer was Frederick Freez, 'a Dutchman and an alien enfranchised', made free of the city in 1497 and in 1506 ordered to dwell upon the common ground at the Rose, otherwise the Bull in Coney Street for ten years; but by 1515 he was living in the parish of St Helen on the Walls in Aldwark. Frederick's son Valentine, free as a cordwainer in 1538, was a Protestant martyr, burned alive on the Knavesmire at the same stake with his wife, a deed attributed by Fuller to Edward Lee, 'the cruel archbishop'. Among later printers in the city the most famous, deservedly, is the eccentric Dubliner Thomas Gent (1693–1778), who settled permanently here in 1724 and took over the noted press in Coffee Yard. Gent left an autobiography, published in 1832, but in his own time was particularly known for his *Antient and Modern History of the famous City of York*, which he brought out in 1730, anticipating Drake by six years. Gent was not a scholar, but in this and his later histories of Ripon and Hull he displayed great powers of detailed observation which have given his work permanent value as a record of much that would otherwise be unknown.

The York trade in books was of immense value, and reached its peak at the Bible in Stonegate under John Todd from 1762 to 1811. Todd, who at first had Henry Sootheran (later Sotheran) as his partner, in 1766 launched a circulating library of several thousand books on all subjects. Subscribers of 3s a quarter or 12s a year could have two books at a time and change them as often as they pleased, but they could have only one new book at a time for up to six days; other books might be kept for a month. Non-subscribers were allowed to borrow books by paying 6d for a copy of the catalogue and at the rate of 1s for a folio, 6d for a quarto, 3d for an octavo and 2d for a duodecimo, for one week, with an extra charge of 3d for a fortnight and 4d for three weeks. This commercial lending library was replaced in 1794 by the Book Society, which grew into the Subscription Library and lasted until 1918. York was slow to adopt the Public Libraries Act, resolutions being defeated by polls of the ratepayers in 1881 and 1887 before winning through in 1891. The first public library, in Clifford Street, was opened by the Duke of York (later King George V) on 4 October 1893.

John Todd had been apprenticed to John Hildyard, an earlier owner of 'The Bible', and stayed on as assistant to Hildyard's successor John Hinxman who at the end of 1759 published the first two volumes of Laurence Sterne's *Tristram Shandy*. No bookseller in London was prepared to take the risk of issuing the book, which was considered ridiculous and unsaleable. Sterne hawked the copy around his acquaintance in York and eventually, as John Croft the wine merchant and antiquary wrote, 'a Mr. Lee a Gent[n] of York and a Bachelor of a liberall turn of mind lent him One

hundred pounds towards the Printing the Work'. Hinxman
sold 200 copies in two days and the great London publisher
Dodsley then agreed to bring the book out, as was announced
in the *London Chronicle* of 1 January 1760. The identity of
Sterne's benefactor, Mr Lee, was for a long time a mystery,
but he has been identified as William Phillips Lee, the
wealthy descendant of an ancient Buckinghamshire family,
who had settled in York by 1760 and died on 12 March
1778 at the age of 71. Lee subscribed to the first volume of
Sterne's sermons, also published in 1760, and eventually
settled in what was then a modern house, No. 40 Blossom
Street, demolished in 1965 in spite of a Building Preservation Order. After his death, Lee's library was said to comprise
many valuable items 'in every class of Literature, and in
most Languages'. Though the catalogue of this sale is lost,
another of the same period shows that the collection of Luke
Thompson, a Micklegate solicitor, included 400 volumes in
English, 300 Latin and Greek, 150 French, 100 in Spanish
and Portuguese, and another 100 in Italian. York society was
not barbaric.

York of the eighteenth century not only appreciated
books: it had also a successful theatre. There had been a
theatre in York for generations, and there had been a
commission as early as 1629 for William Perrey to keep a
company of players to be known as His Majesty's Servants
for the City of York. At the opening of the eighteenth
century plays were staged in the upper room of the Thursday
Market House in what is now St Sampson's Square, and then
in the tottering old hall of the Archbishop's Palace behind
the Minster. The first permanent theatre built for the
purpose was put up in 1744 on the site of the present
Theatre Royal, which has thus had a continuous history of
230 years. This theatre was occupied by Joseph Baker's
Players, so successful that Baker was able in 1764–5 to build
a larger theatre around the old building, without closing.

By good fortune Baker was soon afterwards able to get Tate Wilkinson (1739–1803) as a member of his company, and made him manager in 1768. Wilkinson took over the theatre on Baker's death in 1770, having already obtained for it in the previous year a patent as the Theatre Royal, York. Ever since then the York theatre has been a proving ground for actors and actresses, and has welcomed famous ones, from Mrs Siddons in 1776 onwards. Tate Wilkinson wrote his own life and played himself down with the phrase: 'If I had held my pen but half as well as I have held my bottle, what a charming hand I should have wrote by this time.' But his fame was based on his humanity and honesty as much as on his gifts: when he died it was said that 'owing to his kindness to his performers, his judicious instructions, and his punctuality in pecuniary matters, his dependents considered him more as a father than a master. He excelled both as a tragedian and a mimic, and as a theatrical tutor he was never equalled.'

The diapason closes full on Music, but of the music of York and in York there is no space to write adequately. The Minster has, of course, an immemorial tradition of organs and choir. The first organist of note was John Thorne, a writer of motets and reckoned by Morley as one of his authorities; Thorne died in 1573 and was buried in the nave. The great organ was built in 1632–4 by Robert Dallam, citizen and blacksmith of London, just in time to be heard by Lieutenant Hammond on his visit: 'we saw and heard a faire large high Organ, newly built, richly gilt, caru'd and painted, a deep and sweet snowy Crew of Quiristers . . .' Ten years later the organ was leading the singing against the noise of the Parliamentarian bombardment, so poignantly recollected by Mace in *Musick's Monument*. 'The Enemy had planted their Great Guns so mischievously against the Church . . . that sometimes a cannon bullet has come in at the windows and bounc'd about from pillar to pillar . . .';

but 'they had then a custom in that church (which I hear not of in any other cathedral) which was always before the sermon the whole congregation sang a psalm together with the quire and the organ . . . This organ . . . being let out into all its fulness of stops, together with the quire began the psalm. But when that vast-concording unity of the whole congregational chorus came (as I might say) thundering in, even so as it made the very ground shake under us (Oh the unutterable ravishing soul's delight!) in which I was so transported and wrapt up into High contemplations that there was no room left in my whole man, viz. Body, Soul, and Spirit, for anything below divine and heavenly raptures.'

Conclusion

Modernity is a relative word and shifts perpetually with the march of time. Historical objectivity cannot be achieved in less than three generations or say 100 years and this may excuse us from attempting to follow the story of York and its social and architectural structure beyond mid-Victorian times. But so far little has been said of the great developments of the earlier nineteenth century, when York took another and unexpected twist, at the whim of the Genius Loci, biding its time. In spite of the social and cultural activities of the Georgian period and the great and public-spirited aspirations of many of its citizens, York for a generation after 1800 was a city of much misery and want. After the war-time boom had ended at Waterloo in 1815 the whole country plunged into mass unemployment and a chasm of depression, sliding, with occasional recoveries, towards the Hungry Forties. This was a national graph of a deep-seated disease in the body politic, but the attack was particularly severe in York.

In the remaining streets of the period we see a serene front, of brick or stucco, typically it may be by the design of Peter Atkinson the second and the building craftsmanship of Thomas Rayson the first: South Parade or St

Leonard's Place. Town planning, first exemplified back in the eighteenth century by the street improvements at St Helens churchyard and Blake Street, at Spurriergate and Nessgate, at the foot of Goodramgate and in King's Square, beside St Crux, was beginning to lay hold of York. These changes were marked on the plan published in 1785 by Ann Ward in her abbreviated and revised edition of Drake's *Eboracum*; 'the several places dotted thus ∴∴∴ shew where the Streets have been widened by the public spirit of the Corporation'. Such alterations spread and became the order of the day: the walls, bars, and posterns were threatened, the posterns and three barbicans taken down; in 1806 the Castle moat filled and Castlegate Lane widened; in 1810–20 Ouse Bridge rebuilt; the new House of Correction built on Toft Green. In 1821 Low Ousegate and Spurriergate were widened, in 1827 St Peter's Gate to the Minster Yard was pulled down, in 1831 the Walls breached and St Leonard's Place begun, two years later the grandiose clearance started for the new market place of Parliament Street. All this cost money, yet York did not really have any superfluity of wealth. None the less, great cultural projects were under way: the Yorkshire Philosophical Society was launched in 1822, and in the following year the first of the great Musical Festivals in the Minster (three more were to follow in 1825, 1828, and 1835), in 1825 the City Improvement Commissioners were appointed, in 1827 the York Footpath Association was formed to save and repair the Walls. The area of the Museum Gardens, part of the King's Manor, was granted to the Yorkshire Philosophical Society as a botanical garden and as a site for a museum, and in 1830 the Yorkshire Museum was opened. A year later the British Association for the Advancement of Science was formed, at the suggestion of Sir David Brewster but with the Yorkshire Philosophical Society as its exemplar, and with Canon William Venables Vernon Harcourt of York as its mentor

and first Secretary; the Association acknowledged its
parentage by holding the first meeting, of 1831, in York.

Politically the whole country was in a state of upheaval,
and the Reform Act passed in 1832, to be followed in 1835
by the Municipal Corporations Reform Act, which tore
away the Ainsty and gave it to the West Riding, and abolished
the Old Corporation with its closed shop. This was, in
principle, intended to open the gate to genuinely free
enterprise. Whereas the York Gas Company had laid its
mains in 1823, dissatisfaction at its prices enabled a rival
body to be floated, the York Union Gas-Light Company of
1837. Competition between the two companies lasted for six
years before amalgamation, and brought the rate down from
10s to 6s 8d the 1,000 feet by 1849; but the consumers then
unavailingly pointed out that the average in other towns was
only 4s 6d. York was certainly not altogether a cheap city.
At the same time its population was going up by leaps and
bounds, from under 17,000 in 1801 to 19,000 ten years
later, nearly 22,000 in 1821, over 26,000 by 1831, almost
29,000 in 1841. During the Napoleonic Wars few houses
were built, and overcrowding got a hold, climbing from an
old average of a little under six persons per house to 7·17
in 1811, then declining to a level average of five from 1841
onwards, when the inhabited houses numbered 5,768.

Unlike the greater towns of the West Riding and of the
North generally, York had not been much affected by the
growth of factories and the industrial revolution, but some
side effects began to appear. In 1816 the first steamboat was
put into service between York and Hull and greater changes
were portended, regionally, by the start made on Goole
Docks in 1820. By 1832, two years after the successful
opening of the Liverpool and Manchester Railway, schemes
for railways to York began to be discussed. Three years
later, in the year of the passing of the Old Corporation, the
new age was signalled by the establishment of the York and

North Midland Railway Company. In 1839 the first train ran, and by the summer of 1840 there were four trains to London every day and the journey had been cut to ten hours. By 1842 the last stage coach had run. The rails reached Newcastle in 1844 and Scarborough in 1845. In 1854 a giant amalgamation took place of the lines directly concerned with York traffic, forming the North Eastern Railway, which covered most of Yorkshire, the whole of County Durham, and a great deal else.

This fantastic revolution in transport was due to the march of invention and in Britain was national in scope. There was no real argument about the fact that horse-drawn transport was doomed, whether by road or canal, and that steam traction by rail was speedily to take its place. But there was a whole world of doubt as to where the main lines would run and where the vital junctions would be placed, the ganglia of the trade and industry of the future. In some cases there already existed towns and cities of such overwhelming industrial importance that they were quite inevitably the centres of development: Manchester and Birmingham. In other cases small towns of no special importance became great railway centres: Swindon or Crewe, for example. The case of York was quite different. The city was, economically, in a very poor way and in comparison with Leeds or Hull virtually powerless. It had its historic past and its prestige as the notional second city of the realm and imaginary capital of the North, but in the age of industrial civilisation these counted hardly at all.

The course of history was changed at the crucial moment by one man: George Hudson. The brain and the hand were his, and the weapon of £30,000 of capital was put into his hand by his fortunate legacy of 1827. There is no doubt that Hudson, ambitious as he was, was a fundamentally honest man with a disinterested desire to improve the position of York and of his fellow citizens. Sincere local patriotism has seldom been found in such concentrated form or carried to such extreme lengths. As soon as the possibility of railways appeared on the horizon, Hudson made it his business to learn all about the new form of transport, to meet George Stephenson the engineer and the early promoters in the North. It was upon Stephenson that Hudson urged that he should 'mak all t'railways cum to York', and when Stephenson would have none of it – seeing no value in traffic to the effete city – determined to go it alone. By almost superhuman efforts on committees of the old and new corporations over a period of years, then on the boards of company after company and working at prospectuses and draft bills for Parliament, Hudson achieved his end. York, with no obvious advantages for the part except its position in a level plain, did become the greatest railway centre in its region and the central node on the main route from London to Edinburgh. In a time of frenzied promotion of more railways than the country could hold, or pay for, Hudson promoted almost exclusively lines that made sense. In the course of the general mania he manipulated accounts and cut corners to keep his lines from bankruptcy. When the crash came it was Hudson, as the most prominent figure, that got most of the blame and virtually all of the disgrace; yet he was not fraudulent and was never prosecuted; he was re-elected as MP for Sunderland for another ten years. Many others, some of them a great deal higher up the then strict social scale, were equally blameworthy, but Hudson never named them. Charles Dickens asked a friend why he stuck to Hudson: 'Because he had so many people in his power, and held his peace.' The railways that Hudson promoted did not fail and went on from strength to strength.

George Hudson was an altogether exceptional man, but though the part that he played was essential, he was only one of a number of men who, in the York trade of the nine-teenth century, made their mark. He happened to be a linen-draper, a member of one of the less characteristic businesses of the city. More typical middlemen dealt in butter and bacon, tea and cocoa, confectionery and toys. The butter trade was due to the existence in York of the legal staple: all butter from the Ouse valley as far south as the Wharfe, if packed in firkins for export wholesale, had to be brought to the Butter Market in Micklegate 'to be viewed searched weighed and sealed' and appropriate dues paid. The old butter stand, where this was done, stood on the frontage of the churchyard of St Martin-cum-Gregory and was rebuilt about 1778, to be pulled down fifty years later when the trade had ceased. In Drake's time the export of butter from York was 60,000 firkins a year, rising to 80,000 by 1780 but dropping to less than 15,000 firkins by 1818. The firkin of butter was reckoned at half a hundredweight. The placing of the Butter Market on Micklegate Hill resulted in that area having a concentration of merchants who dealt in dairy products, bacon and provisions.

Dealing in tea, coffee, cocoa and sundries was quite a different business, and most of it was done on the other side of the river. Not the beverages alone were sold over the counter, but commonly also the cups: hence the curious description found in the early directories and in Dr White's plans, of 'Tea and China-man'. A good deal of this trade was in the hands of Quakers, notably the Tuke family. It is not generally realised that the great firm known as Rowntrees came into being through the division of the much older business of the Tukes, founded in the second quarter of the eighteenth century. The tea trade moved to London, and the cocoa and chocolate side was taken over by the brothers Henry Isaac and Joseph Rowntree, sons of Joseph Rowntree the first (1801–59). The old Tuke shop was in Castlegate, not far from the Coppergate premises which housed the later confectionery business of the Craven family. The third great York firm famous for sweets started in 1767 and for two

generations belonged to the family of Baildon or Bayldon.
Later partnerships with Robert Berry of St Helen's Square
and with Joseph Terry led to Terrys, which has continued
under four later generations of the same family.

With perhaps some spiritual kinship to confectionery is the
trade in children's toys, still firmly established in York. By
1798 the description 'toyman' was applied in the Universal
Directory to John Barber of Coney Street, John Bell in
Stonegate who also sold snuff, John Jameson of College
Street, John Lund of Goodramgate, and George Stones of
Spurriergate. By 1823 the number of toy manufacturers and
warehouses had risen to nine, as well as William Morritt of
Feasegate, a toy turner. Of the nine, three others were mainly
wood turners, one a turner of brass, iron and ivory as well as
wood, another a jeweller, one a trunk maker, one a comb
maker and one a basket maker; while Martha Marshall of
16 Coney Street was a manufacturer of fishing tackle,
jewellery, cabinets and spinning wheels.

From the cradle to the grave: York was also a great centre
of monumental masons. Besides the firms of sculptors, such
as the Fishers, there were humbler yards which produced
many hundreds of gravestones and tablets. They and their
products, with the epitaphs inscribed, were studied by J. B.
Morrell in his books *York Monuments* and *The Biography of
the Common Man of the City of York as recorded in his Epitaph*,
probably the first representative collection made for a single
city and running from the Roman period to recent times.
Through the nineteenth century the yards which did most
business were those of Plows at Foss Bridge and Skelton in
Micklegate. There were three generations of Plows, beginning with Benjamin (1765–1824) who worked for twelve
years as a mason at the Minster, and his son William Abbey
Plows (1789–1865). The extremely prolific Matthew
Skelton seems to have been a father (1772–1844) and son
(1798–1878) of the same name, at first at what is now No. 25

on the south side of the street, and later behind No. 64 in the yard running back to Tanner Row.

Some of the masons, to judge from the doggerel, may have composed the verses they inscribed on memorials; others may have been scribbled down by a mourning relative, or simply taken from a volume of poems and slightly mangled, like the odd version of Dryden's Hymn for St Cecilia's Day on the stone at Holy Trinity, Micklegate, to Adam Bowlby who died in 1819. Inside the church on the south wall is a mediaeval inscription to *Walterus Flos*, that is Walter Flower, one of the family of St Robert of Knaresborough (died 1235), son of Took Flower, twice Mayor of York in the earliest days of the mayoralty under Richard Coeur-de-Lion. St Robert, dying elsewhere, has left no monument in York, and this applies to others of her most famous sons: Miles Coverdale, probably born here in 1488, and John Flaxman, certainly, in 1755. In a rather different category of fame is the son of the Skeldergate ferryman Edward Bowling, proved by George Benson and the late Miss Isabel Pressly to have been the Lieutenant in the Royal Navy whose death in 1797 was immortalized by Charles Dibdin's poem:

> *Yet shall poor Tom find pleasant weather*
> *When He who all commands*
> *Shall give to call life's crew together*
> *The word to pipe all hands;*
> *Thus death who Kings and tars despatches*
> *In vain Tom's life hath doff'd;*
> *For tho' his body's under hatches,*
> *His soul is gone aloft.*

Born in York; married in York, like Vanbrugh; died in York: three categories of men, overlapping yet distinct. Many of those born in the city, whether of old families or of mere passing strangers, like Flaxman, go away to live and die elsewhere. Others, not York born, come from afar, like Martin Soza the Spanish goldsmith, born in 'Sapher' (Zafra), free of the city in 1529, chamberlain in 1534 and sheriff in 1545, who was buried in the Minster in 1560. The personal motives of the moves are seldom known, and what we see are glimpses of the unexpected. In our course through the city and its past we have seen again and again that this is the one true constant: in York one may expect nothing but the unexpected. Whatever the future may hold for York, it will come as a surprise.

In the mean time the citizens and all who love the city must remain watchful over her integrity, spiritual and physical, that the character and essence be not lost. We have to bear constantly in mind the noble eloquence of John Philpot Curran: 'The condition upon which God hath given liberty to man is eternal vigilance; which condition if he break, servitude is at once the consequence of his crime, and the punishment of his guilt.' By day or night at all seasons we have to walk the Walls and streets with the York Waits:

Wak'd by a hornpipe pretty, Play'd along York city,
In a winter's night, By moon or lanthorn light,
Through hail, rain, frost or snow, Their rounds the music go;
But, their fingers frost-nipt, So many notes are o'erslipt
That you'd take sometimes The Waits for the Minster chimes:
Then, Sirs, to hear their music
Would make both me and you sick,
And much more to hear a roopy fiddler call
'Past three, fair frosty morn,
Good morrow, my masters all'.

Bibliography and Abbreviations

AASRP	Associated Architectural Societies' *Reports and Papers*
Auden 1906	G. A. Auden ed., *A Handbook to York and District* (British Association, 1906)
Benson 1968	G. Benson, *York* (combined reprint of 3 vols., 1911, 1919, 1925; 1968)
BM	British Museum and Library
	J. Browne, *The History of the Metropolitan Church of St Peter, York*, 2 vols., (1847)
Cal Close R	*Calendar of Close Rolls*
Cal Pat R	*Calendar of Patent Rolls*
	H. Cave, *Antiquities of York* (1813)
	T. P. Cooper, *York: the Story of its Walls, Bars and Castles* (1904)
	——*The History of the Castle of York* (1911)
	——*Literary Associations of the City of York* (1925)
Davies 1868	R. Davies, *A Memoir of the York Press* (1868)

Davies 1880	——*Walks through the City of York* (1880)
Drake 1736	F. Drake, *Eboracum: or the History and Antiquities of the City of York* (1736) revised edition by A. Ward (1785) revised edition by T. Wilson and R. Spence (1788)
EP–NS	English Place-Name Society
EYLHS	East Yorkshire Local History Society
	T. Gent, *The Antient and Modern History of the Famous City of York* (1730)
	J. Halfpenny, *Fragmenta Vetusta, or the Remains of Ancient Buildings in York* (1807)
Hargrove 1818	W. Hargrove, *History and Description of the Ancient City of York* (2 vols. as 3, 1818)
Harvey 1954	J. H. Harvey, *English Mediaeval Architects* (1954)
Heape 1937	R. G. Heape, *Georgian York* (1937)
Knight 1944	C. B. Knight, *A History of the City of York* (1944)
	W. Monkhouse, F. Bedford, and J. Fawcett, *The Churches of York* [1843]
Morrell 1944	J. B. Morrell, *York Monuments* [1944]
Morrell 1948	——*The Biography of the Common Man of the City of York as recorded in his Epitaph* (1947–48)
	——*Woodwork in York* (1949)
	J. E. Morris, *York* (Little Guide, 1924)
Pressly 1938	I. P. Pressly, *A York Miscellany* (2 vols., [1938, c. 1964])
Raine 1955	A. Raine, *Mediaeval York* (1955)
	J. Raine, *York* (Historic Towns, 1893)

RCHM I, II, III   Royal Commission on Historical Monuments, Inventories of the *City of York*:
I *Eburacum: Roman York* (1962)
II *The Defences* (1973)
III *South-West of the Ouse* (1972)
J. Rodgers, *York* (1951)

RS   Rolls Series

SS   Surtees Society

Stacpoole 1972   A. Stacpoole ed., *The Noble City of York* (1972)

VCH *York*   Victoria County History, *City of York* (1961)
R. Willis, *Portrait of York* (1972)

YAJ   *Yorkshire Archaeological Journal* (Yorkshire Archaeological Society)

YASRS   Yorkshire Archaeological Society: Record Series

YAYAS   Yorkshire Architectural and York Archaeological Society

YCA   York City Archives

YCL   York City Library

YCR   *York Civic Records*, ed. A. Raine (YASRS, XCVIII, CIII, CVI, CVIII, CX, CXII, CXV, CXIX, 1939–53)

YML   York Minster Library

YPS   Yorkshire Philosophical Society

Notes to the Text

References are generally given only for facts not to be easily found in the works included in the preceding Bibliography. In the perambulations, Chapters II–IV, use has been made of the recently published inventories of the Royal Commission on Historical Monuments, amplified by personal research in the City Archives (particularly the Registers of Deeds, E. 93–98), in the printed directories, in parish rate books and wills, mostly in the Borthwick Institute, York; and in the York newspapers, remarkably indexed by the City Library.

Page   PREFACE
xii   Size of Cathedrals – see J. H. Harvey, *Cathedrals of England and Wales* (1974), pp 84–8

       Fairfax – it was Ferdinando, 2nd Baron Fairfax of Cameron (1584–1648) who, as governor of York from the capitulation in 1644, secured the safety of York monuments. His more famous son, Thomas the 3rd Baron (1612–71), Parliamentary commander-in-chief from 1645, was also instrumental in protecting York.

Page
xiii   Cooper – note the recent tribute by Dr R. M. Butler
        (RCHM II, 1): Cooper's 'books are so well based
        on archival sources that further research has con-
        firmed rather than corrected his account . . .'

INTRODUCTION

1   'Durham is old . . .'– R. Weatherburn in *The Railway
        Magazine*, XV (July 1904), 26
        Bit ilu Lahmu – *New Catholic Encyclopaedia* (1967),
        II, 373; *Encyclopaedia Britannica* (1971), III, 552
2   Ebrauc – *Histories of the Kings of Britain* by Geoffrey
        of Monmouth, translated by S. Evans (Everyman,
        1912), 26–7, 41, 52, 67, 73–4
        Etymology – E. Ekwall, *Oxford Dictionary of English
        Place-Names* (1936), 519; A. H. Smith, *The Place-
        Names of the East Riding of Yorkshire and York*
        (EP–NS, XIV, 1937), 275–80
4   Richmond – RCHM I, xxix
5   Classicianus – F. Cottrill, *London Wall through
        Eighteen Centuries* (1937), 30–4 in *Antiquaries
        Journal*, XVI, 1–7
15   Floods – H. G. Ramm, 'The end of Roman York' in
        R. M. Butler ed., *Soldier and Civilian in Roman
        Yorkshire* (1971), 181–3
16   Elmet, Barkston Ash, Skyrack – A. H. Smith, *The
        Place-Names of the West Riding of Yorkshire*, iv
        (EP–NS, XXXIII, 1961), 1–3, 88–9
        Barony of Sherburn – W. Farrer ed., *Early Yorkshire
        Charters*, I (1914), 21–3; J. H. Harvey, 'Bishop-
        hill and the Church of York', YAJ, XLI pt. 163
        (1966), 377–93
19   Anglian Tower – J. Radley in YAJ, XLIV (1972),
        38–64
        Welsh poems – ibid., 55 and n.[2]

Page

19 Minster – B. Hope-Taylor, *Under York Minster* (Dean and Chapter of York, 1971)

20 Alcuin – R. Cramp, *Anglian and Viking York* (Borthwick Papers No. 33, 1967), 7–8

CHAPTER I

23 Vikings – A. L. Binns, *The Viking Century in East Yorkshire* (EYLHS, Local History Series No. 15, 1963); M. Dolley, *Viking Coins of the Danelaw and of Dublin* (British Museum, 1965); J. Radley, 'Economic Aspects of Anglo-Danish York', *Medieval Archaeology*, XV (1971), 37–57

27 St Mary ad Valvas – YML, L 1(2), p. 74; BM, Harleian MS. 6971, f. 119

Tombs of archbishops – H. G. Ramm and others in *Archaeologia*, CIII (1971), 101–47

28 St Anthony's Hall – J. S. Purvis and E. A. Gee, *St Anthony's Hall, York* (St Anthony's Hall Publications No. 1, 1953)

32 Gap-tooth demolition – J. H. Harvey, *Conservation of Buildings* (1972), 166–7, 225

Redundant churches – York Redundant Churches Commission, *New Uses for Old Churches* (Church Information Office and S.P.C.K., 1967); and *Supplementary Report* (1969)

35 York 2000 – *York 2000 – People in Protest* (York 2000, 1973)

36 Yorkshire Philosophical Society – YPS, *Annual Report for 1971* (1972)

37 Nursery etc. – J. H. Harvey, 'The Family of Telford, Nurserymen of York', YAJ, XLII pt. 167 (1970), 352–7; 'Points of Garden Interest in and about York', *The Northern Gardener* (Northern Horticultural Society), XXIV No. 5 (Sep 1970), 153–5;

Page

'Garden History in the North', ibid., XXV No. 2
(March 1971), 50–7

CHAPTER II

39   Fairfax – The tomb at Bilbrough is of Thomas, 3rd
Baron; his father, the Fairfax who captured and
spared York, lies at Bolton Percy. Andrew Marvell,
when tutor to Thomas's daughter Mary (later
Duchess of Buckingham) in 1650–2 wrote 'Upon
the Hill and Grove at Bilbrough', a Latin poem too,
the long poem 'Upon Appleton House', Fairfax's
other country seat, his famous 'The Garden', and
others.

40   Dringhouses etc. – the account of buildings to south-
west of the Ouse depends largely on RCHM III,
and the perambulations as a whole owe much to
Davies 1880.

41   William Gray – YCL, YL/Gray, Letters

45–6   Bar Convent etc. – E. A. Gee in RCHM III, 40–7,
63–4, 124

Pritchett – G. H. Broadbent, 'The Life and Work of
Pritchett of York', in W. Singleton ed., *Studies in
Architectural History*, II (1956), 102–24

47   Forest boundary – T. Gill, *Vallis Eboracensis* (1852),
47–9

48   Skelton – H. E. C. Stapleton and M. J. A. Thompson,
Skelton Village (1971)

49   Marygate Tower – R. M. Butler, RCHM II, 169–
71; for the records, and Liberty of St Mary's,
B. A. English and C. B. L. Barr, YAJ, XLII
(1971), 198–235, 359–86, 465–518

51   Wolstenholme – Borthwick Institute, York Preroga-
tive Wills, Reg. 1813, f. 514; see J. H. Harvey,
Sources for the History of Houses (British Records

Page

Association, Archives and the User No. 3, 1975),
44–5

53 Monkgate etc. – H. G. Ramm, YAJ, XLII, 132–5

54 Abbot – his history of York Minster is BM, Stowe
MS. 884; his views of buildings in York are in the
Gott Collection in Wakefield Museum

55 St Maurice House – YML, Sub-Chanter's Book No.
4 (102, 268), f. 77

CHAPTER III

58 Defences – R. M. Butler in RCHM II

59 Wall walks – Drake 1736, 262

60 Fires – J. H. Harvey, YAJ, XLI pt. 163, 365–7

61 Black Friars – C. F. R. Palmer, YAJ, VI (1881),
396–419
Toft Green – Hargrove 1818, II, 178–9

63 Cholera Burial Ground – AASRP, XXXVII, xxiii,
lxxxi; XXXVIII, xxii, lxxiii

68 Ace House – Raine 1955, 297

CHAPTER IV

73 Red Lion – J. H. Harvey, *Sources for the History of
Houses* (above, note to p. 51), 46–8

79 All Saints glass – E. A. Gee, 'The Painted Glass of
All Saints' Church, North Street, York', *Archaeologia*, CII (1969), 151–202

84 Clock – T. P. Cooper, AASRP, XXX.i (1909), 254

86 Spouts – YCA, M. 17 (2 May 1763)
Herb Market – H. Richardson, *The Medieval Fairs
and Markets of York* (St Anthony's Hall Publica-
tions No. 20, 1961), 31
Herbert's House – T. W. French, 'The Herbert
House, York', YAJ, XXXIX, 343–55

Page

89   Ledger – *York Courant*, 19 Aug. 1755; 1 Feb. 1763;
       1 March 1763; 3 Dec. 1765
90   King's Court – K. M. Longley in *Recusant History*,
       XII No. 1 (Jan. 1973), 4–7 and note 42

CHAPTER V

94   Mitley – Davies 1880, 28–9, 177; R. Gunnis,
       Dictionary of British Sculptors (1953), 261
       Hindley – Davies 1880, 21–3; T. P. Cooper, AASRP,
       XXX.i, 250–1
95   Mulberry – YML, Chapter Wills, Reg. 1, f. 33v
       Star Inn – T. P. Cooper, AASRP, XXXIX.ii (1929)
       273–318
       'The Bible' – T. P. Cooper, AASRP, XXXIX.i
       (1928), 83–131
96   Norman house – J. S. Syme, YAYAS *Annual Report
       1951–2*, 36–9
       Minster Gates – T. P. Cooper, *The Sign of the Crown*
       (York, E. Story, 1925)
97   St Michael-le-Belfrey – J. Raine ed., *The Fabric Rolls
       of York Minster* (SS, XXXV, 1859)
       Archbishops' Hall – College of Arms, Arundel MS.
       30, f. 214
       Gardens – W. Brereton, *Travels in Holland*, ed. E.
       Hawkins (Chetham Society, I, 1834), 72–3;
       L. G. W. Legg ed., *A Relation of a Short Survey of
       26 Counties* (Stuart Series, VII, 1904), 20–1
98   Treasurer's House – Mrs E. Gray, *The Mansion
       House of the Treasurers of York Minster* (York, B.
       Johnson, 1933); National Trust, *Treasurer's House*
       (1963); L. P. Wenham, *Gray's Court, York* (n.d., c.
       1965)
99   Bedern – F. Harrison, *Life in a Medieval College*

Page

(1952); F. Harrison, 'The Bedern Chapel, York',
YAJ, XXVII pt. 106 (1923), 197–211

100 Minster – I am indebted to Dr Gee for allowing me to
see, in advance of publication, his account of the
architectural history to 1290, written for the forth-
coming book to be published by the dean and
chapter.

101 John of Waverley – see Harvey 1954, 288

Distortions – D. J. Dowrick and P. Beckmann, 'York
Minster structural restoration', *Proceedings of the
Institution of Civil Engineers*, 1971 Supplement (vi),
93–156

103 Aeneas Sylvius – *Smith College Studies in History*
(Northampton, Mass.), XXII Nos. 1–2 (1936–7),
20–1

104 Richard II – J. H. Harvey in F. R. H. du Boulay
and C. M. Barron ed., *The Reign of Richard II*
(1971), 211, 216

Romanus – Matthew Paris, *Chronica Majora* ed. H. R.
Luard (RS 57), v (1880), 534–5

105 Simon of York – Harvey 1954, as for other York
masters

106 Yellow Stain – J. H. Harvey, *Mediaeval Craftsmen*
(1975), 14–15

Ivo de Raghton – J. H. Harvey, *The Mediaeval
Architect* (1972), 79–80

107 Choir – J. H. Harvey, *Cathedrals of England and
Wales* (1974), 179–80

108 Drawing Office – J. H. Harvey in *40th Annual
Report of the Friends of York Minster for 1968*
(1969), 9–13

111   Viking York – see above, notes to p. 23; also D. Waterman, 'Finds from Late Saxon, Viking, and Early Mediaeval York', *Archaeologia*, XCVII (1959), 59–106; K. M. Richardson, 'Excavations in Hungate, York', *Archaeological Journal*, CXVI (1959), 51–114. On plants and fruits grown or gathered I am grateful to Miss F. E. Crackles for information and comments.

114   Population – J. Raine ed., *Historians of the Church of York* (RS 71, 1879), i, 454; figures of *c.* 1639 from Bodleian, MS. Rawlinson C. 886, kindly communicated by Dr D. M. Palliser

115   Waste – F. W. Brooks, *Domesday Book and the East Riding* (EYLHS, Local History Series No. 21, 1966), 41

   Archbishop's privileges – F. Liebermann, YAJ, XVIII, 412–16; A. F. Leach ed., *Visitations and Memorials of Southwell Minster* (Camden Society, New Series, XLVIII (1891), 190–6; J. Raine ed., *The register . . . of Walter Gray* (SS, LVI, 1872), 232

116   Rate assessments – YCA, E. 70

118   Freemen – F. Collins ed., *Register of the Freemen of the City of York*, 1272–1759 (SS, XCVI, CII, 1897–1900); R. B. Dobson, 'Admissions to the Freedom of the City of York in the later Middle Ages', *Economic History Review*, 2 Series, XXVI No. 1 (Feb. 1973), 1–22

   Taxations – *c.* 1282, YCA, C. 60; 1301–4, YASRS, XXI (1897); 1327, YASRS, LXXIV (1929), 160–71; 1377, YAJ, XLIII, 128–46; 1381, N. Bartlett, *The Lay Poll Tax Returns for the City of*

Page

York in 1381 (East Riding Antiquarian Society, 1953); 1524, YAJ, IV pt. 15 (1876), 170–201

119 List – C. Bonnier, *English Historical Review*, XVI (1901), 501

121 Aliens – Raine 1955, 155–6

122 Mother Shipton – Morrell 1948, 107

Ousegate – VCH *York*, 52

123 Hungate – M. Sellers ed., *York Memorandum Book* (SS, CXXV, 1915), 222

Paving – *Cal Close R 1296–1302*, 218; *Cal Pat R 1317–21*, 395; *1327–30*, 457; *1334–8*, 162; YCA, Memorandum Book B/Y, ff. 48–48b

Street Cleaning – YCR, i, 113; v, 30; viii, 31, 38

124 Nameplates – YPS, William White MS., 'Analecta Eboracensia', p. 7 item 16

Lighting – VCH, *York*, 119

Decline – ibid., 73; *Cal Pat R 1429–36*, 51; YCR, ii, 9–10

Foss Bridge – *Cal Pat R 1405–8*, 171, 366; *1408–13*, 52, 274

125 Coney Street – L. F. Salzman, *Building in England* (1952/1967), 430–2

Quayage – *Cal Pat R 1364–7*, 249 etc.

Guild – R. H. Skaife, *The Register of the Guild of Corpus Christi in the City of York* (SS, LVII, 1872), vi–vii

CHAPTER VII

129 Wills – D. M. Palliser, *The Reformation in York 1534–1553* (Borthwick Papers No. 40, 1971)

130 Chantries – R. B. Dobson, 'The Foundation of Perpetual Chantries by the Citizens of medieval York', *Studies in Church History*, IV (Leiden, Brill, 1967), 22–38

182   *Notes*

Page

130   John Hag – Borthwick Institute, York Wills, Reg. 3,
       f. 307v
133   Duke's Hall – the foundations were dug in 1638
       (RCHM I, 114) and it was presumably finished by
       the outbreak of the Civil War in 1642
       Brick building – YCA, B.36, f. 122b
134   Colouring – ibid., B. 32, f. 249
       Rates, ibid., E. 70–E. 74
135   Descriptions – RCHM III, xxx–xxxi
136   Camden – BM, Cotton MS. Julius F. x, f. 121 etc.
137   Artists – RCHM III, xxxii–xxxvi
138   Fawkes – Pressly 1938, I, 26–9; Raine 1955, 121–2;
       K. M. Longley, 'Three Sites in the City of York',
       Recusant History, XII No. i (Jan. 1973), 1–7
139   Lister – Davies 1868, 107–9
       Buckingham – Drake 1736, 269
140   Carpenter – R. Gunnis, *Dictionary of British Sculptors*
       (1953), 82; Morrell 1944, 39–40, 121

CHAPTER VIII

143   Richard II – see above, note to p. 104
144   Development – Knight 1944; VCH *York*
       Medicine – Pressly 1938, 141–57, 210–13; Auden
       1906, 241–2, 230–1; M. C. Barnet, 'James
       Atkinson, Surgeon 1759–1839', YPS *Annual
       Report for 1971* (1972), 48–9
145   Millington – Drake's additions to his own copy of
       Eboracum (p. 33) in YCL
       Stubbs – B. Taylor in *George Stubbs: Rediscovered
       Anatomical Drawings* (Arts Council, 1958), 6–7
146   Gowland, Garencieres, Atkinson – Auden 1906, 233,
       232, 228
147   The Retreat – W. K. and E. M. Sessions, *The Tukes
       of York* (London, Friends House, 1971)

Page

147 Horners – L. P. Wenham, 'Hornpot Lane and the Horners of York', YPS *Annual Report for 1964*, 25–56

148 Clockmakers – T. P. Cooper, 'The Old Clockmakers and Watchmakers of York', AASRP, XXX.i (1909), 243–60

Silversmiths – C. Oman, 'The Civic Plate and Insignia of the City of York'; 'The Plate of the City Companies of York', *The Connoisseur*, CLXVI (Oct–Dec 1967), 71–3, 139–43, 222–4; T. M. Fallow and H. B. McCall, *Yorkshire Church Plate* (Leeds, YAS, 1912–15), I, 339–53

Bell-founders – G. Benson, *The Bells of the Ancient Churches of York* (York, W. Pickwell, 1885); 'York Bellfounders', AASRP, XXVII. ii (1904), 623–49

Iron-founders – R. J. Malden, 'Railings', York Civic Trust, *Annual Report 1971–72*, 12–14

149 Druggists – Knight 1944, 586–7, 622–3, 676, 717–18

150 Holborne – YCA, D.14, 152; Poll books 1807, 1820; *York Gazette*, 11 Feb. 1837

Gardens – see note above to p. 37; Benson 1968, III, 70, 75; YCL, records of the Ancient Society of York Florists

Artists – G. Benson, 'John Browne 1793–1877',

152 YPS, *Report 1918*; T. P. Cooper, *The Caves of York* (York Art Gallery, 1934); J. Ingamells in Stacpoole 1972

153 Fisher – Advertisement of Richard Fisher, *York Journal*, 15 July 1746; York newspaper files and parish registers; information kindly supplied by Miss C. Myerscough

154 Carr – Davies, YAJ, IV pt. 15 (1876), 202–13;

Page

pedigree from College of Arms, YCL, Y929. 1; YCA, E. 93, 268; E. 94, f. 75

155   Craftsmen – information on families compiled from deeds, wills, parish registers and York newspapers; see G. Beard, *Georgian Craftsmen and their Work* (1966)

156   Freez – Davies 1868, 7–15, 341; A. G. Dickens, *Lollards and Protestants in the diocese of York 1509–1558* (1959), 30–3. I am grateful to Dr D. M. Smith for his help in connection with the Protestant Martyrs.

Gent – Pressly 1938, 178–88

157   Lee – J. H. Harvey, 'A Lost Link with Laurence Sterne', YAJ, XLII pt. 165 (1968), 103–7

158   Theatre – Heape 1937, 1–35; Knight 1944, 593–4

159   Music – Knight 1944, 626–7

CONCLUSION

163   Gas – Knight 1944, 623–4, 674–5

166   Butter – Drake 1736, 220; Hargrove 1818, II, 173–4; Knight 1944, 519–20, 585

168   Tom Bowling – Pressly 1938, II, 23–6

169   York Waits – W. Chappell, *Popular Music of the Olden Time* (1859), II, 549

INDEX

There are collected entries for: Architects, Artists and Craftsmen and, under York, for Inns and Public Houses. Numerals in *italics* are principal references; those in **heavy** type refer to the figure numbers on the plates or (with **p.**) to the pages on which line-blocks occur. The following abbreviations are used: abp, Archbishop of York; (L)M, (Lord) Mayor of York; MP, Member of Parliament.